Native advertising. Content marketing. Branded content. One and the same or totally different? Mike Smith offers an up-close and personal look at today's advertising strategies, how they work, and what we as professionals should and shouldn't be doing. A good read and highly recommended.

—Moira Forbes
Executive Vice President, Forbes Media

When is a news or feature story not a news or feature story? In a world that now blends editorial and advertising, the answer can be somewhat muddy. Smith's timely new book explores the native advertising phenomenon from all sides and is a must-read for advertisers, marketers, consumers, and at business schools.

—John Taysom
Visiting Professor, UCL, Cofounder, Privitar

Was there native advertising before the Internet? Mike does a great job of looking at examples from the history of advertising to share with readers as well as examining who is doing what now. Educational, informational, and totally on point, *The Native Advertising Advantage* is just what the frenetic business space needs now—a reminder to slow down, think, implement, and understand.

—Jim Spanfeller
Founder and CEO, Spanfeller Media Group,
The Daily Meal, and The Active Times

Mike Smith does a wonderful service to the world of publishing, as well as to the consumer, as he digs deep into the new avenues advertisers and publishers take. He educated us with *Targeted* and takes us even further with *The Native Advertising Advantage*, which is a very well-thought-out and accessible read. On the cutting edge as always, I look forward to what Mike will bring us next.

—Stephen M. R. Covey
New York Times bestselling author of *The Speed of Trust* and coauthor of *Smart Trust*

Native advertising is a complex and sometimes controversial segment of the media industry, and Smith does a great job of cutting through the confusion and exploring the differences between advertising, native advertising, and content marketing. A must-read for all industry insiders, interested consumers, and any business school student interested in media and marketing.

—Steve Forbes
Chairman and Editor in Chief, Forbes Media

When are ads not ads? When they provide useful information to the consumer. However, when they look like a news or feature story, their purpose can be misleading. Let Mike Smith take you on a journey that explores the new world of native advertising—the good and the sometimes controversial. A more experienced guide you will never find.

—David J. Moore
Chairman, Xaxis, and President, WPP Digital

Mike Smith brings decades of knowledge and experience to the table when he talks about advertising and the digital publishing industry. He now tackles native advertising, which is a phenomenon often misunderstood by both industry insiders and consumers looking in from the outside. This book offers a clear, concise look at the industry.

—Troy Young
President, Hearst Magazines Digital Media

Smith sets out to explain the ins and outs of digital advertising to insiders and the general public. Always fact filled, with a historical context, *The Native Advertising Advantage* once again hits a home run.

—Hayley Romer
Chief Revenue Officer, *The Atlantic*

The roller coaster ride of today's media industry poses never-ending challenges to executives and marketers. Fortunately, Michael Smith is always there to guide us . . . this time through the complexities of native advertising. This is the perfect book at the perfect time . . . read it now!

—Roger McNamee
Tech and media investor

Mike Smith's *The Native Advertising Advantage* hit me like watching a flare gun being shot at sea. All consumers—and those who place the ads to excite, entice, and kick them into action—need to read this book. It makes one immediately aware of the unbelievably fast evolution of media—and shows how the blending of true editorial content with that which is paid for is sometimes hard to discern. This book will make everyone on both sides smarter and more aware.

—John "Jay Jay" French
Twisted Sister founder, musician, artist, manager, producer, writer, motivational speaker, and charter member, Long Island Music Hall of Fame

THE NATIVE ADVERTISING ADVANTAGE

BUILD AUTHENTIC CONTENT THAT REVOLUTIONIZES DIGITAL MARKETING AND DRIVES REVENUE GROWTH

MIKE SMITH

New York   Chicago   San Francisco   Athens   London   Madrid
Mexico City   Milan   New Delhi   Singapore   Sydney   Toronto

1 2 3 4 5 6 7 8 9   LCR   22 21 20 19 18 17

ISBN   978-1-259-83568-1
MHID   1-259-83568-5

e-ISBN 978-1-259-83569-8
e-MHID   1-259-83569-3

McGraw-Hill Education books are available at special quantity discounts to use as premiums and sales promotions or for use in corporate training programs. To contact a representative, please visit the Contact Us pages at www.mhprofessional.com.

For my loving and supportive wife, Denise,
and for our wonderful children, Jessica and Michael.

CONTENTS

CONTENTS

FOREWORD

There's no question that we will look back on the 2010s as a moment that the world, and the way we interact, changed forever, a by-product of the unprecedented global penetration of mobile technology. As we approach the tenth anniversary of the iPhone, it is hard to imagine our lives before Steve Jobs stood on that stage and in his trademark, offhanded style, said, "Oh, and there's one more thing we want to share," as he introduced a device that would quickly become indispensable to millions. In addition to changing how we shop (Amazon), date (Tinder), share our happiest events and memories (Facebook, Instagram), get from place to place in our communities (Uber), the rapid rise of smartphone ownership has also changed human behavior, effectively rewiring our brains.

It's a lot like Pavlov's dogs—a case of classical conditioning. The relationship we have with our mobile devices is, in many cases, an addictive one. Eighty-three percent of millennials sleep with phones within reach. In one study of young adults, 29 percent of respondents said they would rather give up sex for three months instead of exchanging their smartphone for a "dumb phone" for a single week. In increasing numbers, young people don't go to movie theaters, as the thought of sitting in a darkened room for 90 minutes causes anxiety and FOMO—fear of missing out (being away from social media for an hour and a half . . . impossible!). And it's not just millennials: IKEA in Asia recently introduced a hotplate that won't turn on until people place their cell phones underneath it, encouraging conversation over dinner. The smartphone addiction knows no age limits.

Along with everything else, mobile devices are reshaping advertising. Apple and Samsung aside, the world's marketers didn't invent cell phone addiction, but it is now their job to form-fit their advertising and communications around all changes in consumer behavior. And that's why we will also look back on this period as a time when native advertising reshaped how consumers engage with brands and marketing messages.

As Mike Smith points out, native advertising has effectively been around for decades. In the 1940s, Texaco sponsored Texaco Star Theater on radio and television and introduced the country to Milton Berle. Newspapers have produced and published sponsored supplements for years, and magazines have long created "advertorials" (one of the worst names ever, in my opinion).

Until recently, native advertising was practiced only by a handful of media outlets. There were a relatively small number of television network owners, ditto for a finite number of newspapers and magazines. These sectors had high barriers to entry around their businesses: their form factor (over-the-air television signals, large printing presses for newspapers, glossy paper and slick design for magazines) limited the number of brand players, as well as innovation and evolution of the medium.

Smartphones level the playing field. The form factor—content presented on a five-inch screen—puts all publishers (initially) on an equal footing. A start-up in Mountain View can easily mimic the look and feel of a brand of stature like the *New York Times*. Or a group of video producers in Williamsburg can create video on par with what NBC creates at 30 Rock. The five-inch screen is the great leveler of content presentation, a historic change from the time when a media company required antennas, broadcast licenses, printing presses, delivery trucks, and more.

But while consumers enjoy myriad content options, the smartphone has presented marketers with an enormous challenge: advertising, as it had always been known, doesn't function the same way on that small screen. The clear demarcation of advertising and editorial presents unique challenges. When people are checking their phones nearly 150 times a day, how do you engage them, as they constantly dart in and out of content?

Native advertising—so smartly defined, chronicled, and dissected by Mike Smith in the following pages—represents a material part of the future of the advertising business. In developed nations, smartphone penetration approaches 70 percent (Pew Research Center report).[1] In some developing nations, where smartphone ownership is skyrocketing, there are regions where there are more people with smartphones than indoor plumbing.

Tens of thousands of publishers—with the upstarts for the first time on the same playing field as the media industry giants— are making new rules for native advertising, breaking them apart when needed, and creating even newer ones.

Here at Hearst, we have the advantage of Mike Smith's creative and analytical mind, helping to drive our business forward every day. We are blessed with one of the highest-functioning, and most profitable, digital publishing operations in the industry, and

Mike is a big part of that success. In *The Native Advertising Advantage*, you will benefit from Mike's understanding of the history of this form of communication, his account of how smart publishers are experimenting today, and most importantly, why unlocking native advertising gives publishers and marketers a strong foundation for future growth.

I enjoyed this book immensely, and hope you will as well.

David Carey
President, Hearst Magazines

INTRODUCTION

Have you ever clicked on one of those online "articles" that just seemed to grab your attention—while you're doing something else on your computer, tablet, or smartphone? For example, I was conducting research online when I read the headline, "What's YOUR Marketing Doing?" with a picture of two men in shirts and ties staring at a computer screen, seemingly in awe. When I clicked on it, I watched a one-minute video showing what was mesmerizing these execs: clicks on their website were up dramatically, which led them to make a quick series of decisions, to ramp up purchasing, production, and shipping: "I need more trucks!" "More shipping containers!" "More trees!" It turns out the product is encyclopedias—that's right, old-fashioned, bulky print encyclopedias—which you can't even donate to Goodwill anymore (literally), because there's no market and no buyers for them, not even for pennies. At the end of the video, we see a baby with a tablet computer, pressing "Buy Now" on the company's webpage, over and over and over. Cute baby, clever video—especially since the company that created it found a new way to induce me to watch it. Of course, the real punch line is from the video's creator, Adobe, which again asks the title question, "Do you know what your marketing is doing? We can help."

This promoted video, positioned seamlessly within the editorial content of an online publication, is an example of *native advertising*—a new way for companies to get your attention, with advertising that doesn't *look* like advertising. Native advertising is information provided not by objective journalists but by savvy marketers; these ads "go native" by blending in with their surrounding editorial content, thus blurring the traditional "church/ state" divide of editorial vs. advertising, which is what makes native advertising so effective. According to the *Harvard Business Review*,[1] "70% of people say they'd rather learn about products through content rather than through traditional advertising."

Moreover, it's not only social media sites like Facebook and Twitter, or even BuzzFeed, that feature native advertising. Serious, mainstream publications like the *New York Times* and the *Washington Post* are embracing native advertising as the newest form of digital revenue.

As an executive in digital media at Hearst—which publishes such well-known magazines as *Cosmopolitan*, *Esquire*, and *Good Housekeeping* (and many more)—I see daily how native advertising is making serious inroads into how advertisers advertise. At the same time, many people in the media industry—even those in marketing, advertising, and communications—don't really know what precisely native advertising is. *Ad Age* explored this dilemma with an article entitled "Is It Content or Is It Advertising?"[2] which contends that content marketing, a category related to native advertising, comprises anywhere from $26.5 billion to $313 billion worldwide (!), depending on what's considered "content marketing." The U.S. market comprised more than $67 billion in 2014—which is enormous when you consider that the

U.S. TV market is around $70 billion. Despite these huge numbers, the article's main focus elaborates on a quote from Procter & Gamble's global brand officer that the term *content marketing* is "overused and under-defined."[3]

While I was publishing my last book about the paradigm shift in digital advertising technology called *Targeted: How Technology Is Revolutionizing Advertising and the Way Companies Reach Consumers*, another paradigm shift in digital advertising was also occurring called native advertising. Native advertising is a complex, controversial topic, yet it's still in its infancy, and publishers are still figuring out how best to handle it. The government is now paying attention because it's concerned that consumers are being deceived by "unsavory marketing practices" that publishers are complicit in. Because of all the issues surrounding native advertising, I saw a need for a comprehensive book about it—from an insider's perspective—which I knew I could provide. While there are how-to books on the topic, that's not what my book is. *The Native Advertising Advantage* isn't about how to develop or sell a native advertising program. Instead, this book describes the growth of native advertising and the implications—actual and potential—of adopting it. My rationale for writing this book, which followed the same approach I'd taken in *Targeted*, is to chronicle the innovations and the innovators who have developed and advanced the marketplace for native advertising and branded content.

I'm fascinated by how native advertising is developing. I'm an industry insider, and I wrote this book because I believe it needed to be written. I couldn't find anything out there that explores native advertising in an accessible way. Native advertising is complicated, and if I can do a good job of untangling the complexity and explaining it with clarity, that helps everybody. That's my goal with this book.

This book will, I hope, eliminate the confusion over all the new terminology—first, by delineating the difference between content marketing and native advertising, then by defining what native advertising is, how it works, how it's used, the ethics and legality of it, and how effective it is. To reveal all that, *The Native Advertising Advantage* provides information gleaned from dozens of interviews with advertisers, marketers, software developers, journalists, and publishers at a broad cross-section of companies to find out how native advertising fits into their marketing mix and ad budget—and how it has paid off. No other book has done this—which is surprising, when you consider these facts:

- When native advertising is compared to traditional display ads, native advertising is more effective: 25 percent more consumers looked at sponsored (branded)[4] articles than display ad units.[5]
- By 2021, native display ad revenue in the United States, which includes native in-feed ads on publisher properties and social platforms, will make up 74 percent of total U.S. display ad revenue, up from a 56 percent share in 2016.[6]
- Native advertising spending in the United States is expected to increase from $1.3 billion in 2013 to $9.4 billion in 2018.[7]
- 40 percent of publishers expect native advertising to drive a quarter or more of their digital revenue.[8]

- 73 percent of 2,000 marketers surveyed were either completely unfamiliar or hardly familiar with native advertising, and only 3 percent claimed to be very knowledgeable.[9]

This book will provide an in-depth analysis of this latest trend in advertising.

However, you don't have to read *The Native Advertising Advantage* sequentially if you don't want to. The chapters are fairly stand-alone, so if you feel, say, that you know (without the slightest doubt) what native advertising is, you might decide to skip Chapter 1. Or, if you're eager to find out what the "best practices" in the industry are, it's OK to turn immediately to Chapter 8. That said, there is useful information and insights in every chapter, but feel free to dip into whichever topic grabs your interest first.

On the other hand, if you want to learn as much as you possibly can about native advertising, I suggest you start at the beginning—to get a clear definition, from a variety of people interviewed for this book, of what native advertising is and how it works. Let's take a look.

CHAPTER 1

WHAT IS NATIVE

ADVERTISING?

The first order of business in this book is to describe what native advertising is—and what it *isn't*. This is critical, because there's still considerable confusion regarding terminology. Native advertising is primarily thought of in digital form, though it's also seen in traditional print magazines and newspapers and even on TV. But online is where it's used most often.

In the earlier days of print journalism—which was not so long ago, because the world is changing at a furious pace—there was a "Chinese wall" between the editorial side of journalism and the advertising side. What that meant was that the journalists who were writing for the publication—whether it was a newspaper, magazine, or any other type of daily, weekly, monthly, or any other periodical publication—wrote articles about their subjects while, separately, salespeople sold advertising in those publications. The idea behind the Chinese wall was that "never the twain should meet." In other words, if there was a scandal brewing at XYZ company and a journalist at The Daily was writing about it, the fact that XYZ had bought a full-page ad from The Daily shouldn't affect what the journalist wrote about that scandal.

That Chinese wall still exists, but native advertising has made it harder to see. That's not just my opinion, though; take a look at some of the definitions I heard while researching this book:

- "Native advertising is basically content that is made to seem as though it is written by a journalist, but is not. It is written by a marketer or an advertiser and is displayed on a website as though it were, in fact, an editorial or a story."[1]
- "Some people think native advertising means advertorials. Other people think it starts with advertorials, but it has

a much wider range. Any ad that fits into the form and function of an application [is] a native ad."[2]

- "The definition of native itself is so nebulous. It's not only sponsored content." Facebook, Twitter, Medium, Spotify, and many other online media companies have "figured out a way to include a brand message as a part of the content experience, and that experience is not always a sponsored content experience."[3]
- "In some ways, I don't even know what native advertising is . . . and in other ways, it's a very old-school idea." This person felt that native ads were just the latest version of old-fashioned advertorials or mat features (articles written by PR folks to fit the dimensions of the newspapers the PR folks were targeting for those articles; in that way the newspaper editors could simply insert those features without having to edit or crop them in any way). "The execution is new, but frankly, a lot of my experiences as a consumer of native advertising have been very frustrating."[4]
- "We define native as anything that looks and feels like it's a part of the page. It doesn't sit off to the side like a little billboard, like banner ads do."[5]

I could list more, but you get the idea: everyone interviewed for this book had a definition of native advertising . . . but those definitions varied a lot.

Some people credit Fred Wilson for the first use of the term "native" in the context of advertising in a speech he gave at an Online Media, Marketing, and Advertising conference. Wilson cofounded Union Square Ventures, a New York City–based venture capital firm that has invested in Twitter, Tumblr, Foursquare, and Kickstarter, among others. Wilson said something to the effect of "Companies are building their monetization strategies in a way that's native to their platform."

Wilson didn't specifically use the term "native advertising"; Dan Greenberg, founder and CEO of Sharethrough, is generally credited with "evangelizing" the concept.[6] When interviewed for this book, Greenberg said, "For years, the way we described our company had been a mouthful: 'technology that powers noninterruptive, content-driven, integrated, respectful, choice-based ads that fit in.' When I heard Fred say the word 'native,' I e-mailed our executive staff that day and told them *native advertising* is the phrase we've been looking for. The next day, we aligned everything we did around the concept of native advertising. We bought the domain name nativeadvertising.com and our team has been publishing content there for years."

Greenberg went on to say that Sharethrough and BuzzFeed were the major players back in the early days of native. (I'll cover more about the origin, history, and growth of native advertising in Chapter 2, but I mention this here because it's relevant to getting to a universal definition of what native advertising really is.) BuzzFeed was the publisher that was publishing many of the early native ads, and Sharethrough was the ad tech company that powered native advertising for other publishers.

So what led to Sharethrough's definition? Greenberg explained, "Native advertising does not just mean sponsored (promoted) posts, though in 2013/2014, that's what people thought. Our original definition of native advertising was 'a form of paid media that follows the form and function of the site or user experience that it lives within.' I've been saying that phrase for years now, and was happy to see the Interactive Advertising Bureau adopt that as the guiding principle in the official native advertising guidelines that they published in 2013.' "

In case you're wondering what the difference is between native advertising and sponsored posts, here's an explanation that should make things a bit clearer: "[Sponsored] posts . . . contain links that point to the home page or specific product pages of the website of the sponsor for which the blogger receives compensation in the form of money, products, services or in other ways."[7]

Once I had at least something basic to go on, I wanted to know more. Greenberg cochaired a task force that worked to codify what native advertising is. The task force operated under the auspices of the Interactive Advertising Bureau (IAB). So even before interviewing Greenberg for this book, I looked at the work the IAB did on the subject

First, a little background. The IAB was founded in 1996 as a trade industry association that currently comprises more than 650 media and technology companies that sell most of the online advertising in the United States (86 percent, to be specific, according to the IAB website). In 2013, the IAB convened the task force that Greenberg was part of to clarify what native advertising is and to provide some guidelines on how native ads should be presented and disclosed. (FYI, we'll address disclosure guidelines further in Chapter 4, which covers ethics and legal issues as well as more regulated guidelines from the FTC, the United States Federal Trade Commission.) The IAB task force included more than 100 companies. You can read the entire 19-page document yourself, but the gist of it is that the IAB identified and defined six major types of native advertising:

1. ***In-feed ad units.*** These are ads *located within* the website's normal content well. They may have been written by or in partnership with the website publisher's team. They are designed to match the surrounding stories. Here are a few examples of BuzzFeed's in-feed ad unit's sponsored articles:
    *   "9 Things That Have Changed in the Last 20 Years" (Brand: Motorola, published April 1, 2014)
    *   "13 Things You'll Miss Most from Your Twenties" (Brand: TV Land, published March 16, 2015)
    *   "10 Feelings All NYC Girls Have at Least Once" (Brand: HBO, published January 6, 2014)
    *   "15 Bands That Probably Wouldn't Exist Without Led Zeppelin" (Brand: Spotify, published December 30, 2013)[8]

2. ***Search ads.*** These are ads usually found *above* the organic search results. They look just like the other results on the page, *except* they are identified as ads. For example, Google places the word "ad" adjacent to the web address of the paid post.

3. ***Recommendation widgets.*** Although the ad is part of the site's content, it doesn't look like the editorial content. It is delivered through a *content link* or widget. It is generally recognizable by words like "you might also like" or "elsewhere from around the web" or "you may have missed" or "recommended for you." A typical

recommendation widget can be found on the right-hand side and/or bottom of articles on publisher websites under the heading "You May Like." Taboola and Out-brain are two of the major providers of this type of native advertisement.

4. *Promoted listings.* Websites that carry these ads are typically not content based; usually they are e-commerce sites. Promoted listings appear identical to the products or services offered on that site. Amazon, for example, labels its promoted listings as "Sponsored Products Related to This Item"; they may appear on Amazon search results, related product detail pages, or elsewhere on the site. Shoppers click through to product pages where they can find information about (and buy) those products.

5. *In-ad (IAB standard).* This "is an ad in a standard IAB container [for example, 300 × 250 or 300 × 600 pixel banners and other display ads] that contains contextually relevant content [information related to the content on that page] within the ad, links to an offsite page, has been sold with a guaranteed placement, and is measured on brand metrics (interaction and brand lift)."[9] For example, an ad promoting Target on allrecipes.com might alert viewers that all the ingredients can be found at their neighborhood store.

6. *Custom/can't be contained.* These are native ads that don't fit in the other categories because they are designed specifically for the particular platform on which they appear. "Examples include Spotify and Pandora's sponsored playlists, as well as Flipboard's signature native ads."[10]

The IAB Task Force provides a framework for evaluating whether something conforms to one of these six categories. And it provides examples from a variety of websites, including (of course) Facebook, Google, YouTube, Twitter, LinkedIn, Buzz-Feed, the Huffington Post, Instagram, Amazon, and others. My favorite comment in the entire report is in the Introduction: " 'What is native advertising?' is a question that the industry has, *almost frantically*, been looking to answer since the term was first coined."[11] The report's most telling point is that "to a large extent, native is in the eye of the beholder," with the caveat that "depending on where one sits in the ecosystem and the strategic and media objectives of the marketer." It does, however, offer a definition:

> [P]aid ads that are so cohesive with the page content, assimilated into the design, and consistent with the platform behavior that the viewer simply feels that they belong.[12]

However, I'm still not sure that definition suffices.

WHAT'S THE DIFFERENCE BETWEEN "NATIVE ADVERTISING" AND "SPONSORED POSTS"?

As mentioned, Dan Greenberg of Sharethrough was one of the people who worked with Susan Borst, senior director of industry initiatives for the IAB, and others at the IAB on the organization's white paper that describes what native advertising is. As he put it,

"I was happy to see the industry come together and put a flag in the ground around what is and what is not native."

Greenberg and his cofounder Rob Fan started Sharethrough in 2008 with the premise that "ads should fit in." The team looked at a variety of advertisements that were appearing on different sites and recognized that the highest-performing ads were the ones that fit in naturally. Early native ad formats included promoted videos on YouTube, promoted tweets on Twitter, and in-feed ads on Facebook, among other types. Greenberg believes Sharethrough was the first company to tie all the various types of ads together because, as he put it, "We realized that these weren't 10 different, disparate ad strategies, but in fact, a theme had emerged, which was that all these ad formats are native to the platform that they live on." In the end, Greenberg believes that while there may be differences among the six types of native ads, they share the same basic characteristics. It's one format, one form of native ad, thus, only ads that are presented in media formats *and* are bought and sold as media *and* fit the form and function of the site or user experience *and* are created by the publisher site can be considered native ads.

Greenberg says a promoted tweet (a Twitter post advertising a third party's product or service) or a promoted playlist on Spotify are, in fact, native ads because they match the form and function of the sites and advertisers pay to promote them. Similarly, an in-feed ad that clicks to a video is native and not a sponsored post.

According to Greenberg, a sponsored post is a piece of content that becomes an ad when some entity pays to promote that post; it becomes a native ad only if it meets all the requirements of a native ad format.

For example, he explained, if you pay Forbes to create a post, but then don't actually promote it anywhere, it's not really an ad. It's as if Forbes was acting as a creative advertising agency. The ad exists, but you never actually did anything with it, so *it's not really an ad until you pay to promote it.* Once you pay Forbes to promote it on its site, it's a native ad. The creation of the sponsored post is not the ad; it's the promotion of the ad. The magic of native advertising is that the advertiser's story doesn't get relegated to the corner of the page, and therefore perceived as a foreign object, but rather, its story gets presented naturally in the feed of other content, and is treated with the same attention and respect as the surrounding stories.

WHAT'S THE DIFFERENCE BETWEEN "NATIVE ADVERTISING," "CONTENT MARKETING," AND "BRANDED CONTENT"?

There is also confusion pertaining to the name "native advertising." Is it the same as "sponsored content"? As "branded content"? As "content marketing"? To answer those questions, I first wanted to see how Wikipedia defined these terms. Here's what I found:

- "*Native advertising* is . . . disguised advertising . . . that matches the form and function of the platform upon which it appears. In many cases, ... an article or video."[13]
- "*Branded content* is a form of advertising that uses the generating of content as a way to promote the

particular brand which funds the content's production. . . . BMW sponsored "The Hire," a series of
short films . . . BMW was the real star."

- **Sponsored content** is not yet defined on Wikipedia.
  The term redirects you to "native advertising."
- **Content marketing** "is . . . the creation and sharing of
  media and publishing content in order to acquire and
  retain customers . . . news, video, white papers, ebooks,
  infographics, case studies, how-to guides, question and
  answer articles, photos, etc."[14]

What then of the difference between branded content and
native advertising? Several of the people interviewed for this book
felt that *native advertising* refers specifically to the *placement* of
the material, not the material itself, which is actually the *branded
content.*

On the other hand, Todd Haskell, SVP and chief revenue
officer for Hearst Magazines Digital Media, sees the terms as
interchangeable, but prefers the term *branded content* to *native
advertising* because "branded content is trying to deliver an
advertiser's message and key value proposition in a manner that
is consistent with [the publisher's] own journalistic standards.
[With branded content], we use everything we know about how
to engage with millions of readers every month, and we leverage
those on behalf of an advertiser."

Meredith Levien, the EVP and chief revenue officer of the
New York Times Company, sees it differently: "Native advertising is just advertising that follows the form of the surrounding
environment and uses the basic capabilities of the surrounding

environment, the same way other providers of content use those capabilities. . . . Branded content is marketers' storytelling or other forms of expression that go beyond traditional campaign advertising: they're two different things. Native advertising is a format, and branded content is one of the things that can go into that format."

Adam Shlachter, president, VM1 at Zenith Media, agrees that branded content is a form of native advertising. To him, native advertising is advertising that fits into a unique format specific to the environment or the platform on which it is placed. It could be a "promoted offer that you would find in something like Foursquare . . . or [a] personalized search result that you find in Google"; "it can be a mobile [app] for video . . . [or a] piece of content . . . that runs inside Forbes platform. The way I see it, native advertising [is] something that's created to reach people in a distinct way that's unique to the platform [on which] they're consuming it."

Steve Piluso, an advertising executive who has held positions in several global media and digital marketing communications companies, perhaps summed up these perspectives when he said, "There are so many different definitions of what this stuff is, and so many points of view . . . if you show something to 10 people, you'll get an equal distribution of people who refer to it as 'native advertising' and people who refer to it as 'brand' or 'branded content.' I think that's where a lot of the confusion comes in."

Reuters' Felix Salmon offered a perspective I'd seen nowhere else, when he described the difference between sponsored (i.e.,) branded content and native ads this way: "Native content tends to aspire more to going viral"[15] and generally to get shared more, all over the web, which display advertising could never do.

All very interesting, and a lot of food for thought. I kept searching. In addition to journalists, publishers, marketers, and advertisers, I wanted to hear from people who develop the software to run native advertising, who said they "pretty much leave the definition to the publisher."[16] They feel that native advertising includes "sponsored content"—that is, content that's created by an advertiser that is then published by the publisher, as well as content that's written by an editorial team that takes its cues from the advertiser. (This suggests to me that when you search the term "sponsored content" on Wikipedia, it should redirect you to "branded content" instead of "native advertising.") Either or both is OK with the software developers; all they're doing is making it possible for an online publication to feature native ads. The whole point of native advertising is that a brand marketer's message should look and feel like any other piece of content. A group of start-ups came forward to provide technology, pipes, and the required software to facilitate and scale native advertising. The primary concern of these companies is that the advertising should "blend seamlessly into the content experience."[17]

However, some former news journalists feel that in the past (e.g., in the early 2000s or so), sponsored content (as compared to branded content) was considered "real content. . . . It was real journalism that was edited, fact-checked, and self-checked, and was produced by people at [the magazine or newspaper]."[18] It was sponsored content because the advertiser's ads ran adjacent to the editorial content and were the only ads to appear with that content. In contrast, content that was created by advertisers *wasn't* reviewed, or fact-checked, or edited by people who worked on a magazine's or newspaper's copydesk. Instead, that content came straight from the advertisers or the brand, and it was basically turnkey.

Even today, when you look at a site like Forbes.com, for instance, you'll find there are three sources of content. One source is the staff of Forbes. Another source is Forbes's "contributors," and these articles or columns include a disclaimer, if you will, that reads: "Opinions expressed by Forbes' contributors are their own." In other words, these columns or articles are essentially opinion pieces, and the disclaimer indemnifies the publication. That said, the contributors have strong credentials—for example, James M. Clash, who writes for Forbes about extreme adventure and those who do it, also writes for *Bloomberg Businessweek*, *Huffington Post*, and the *New York Times*, among others, and is the author of two books, *Forbes to the Limits* and *The Right Stuff: Interviews with Icons of the 1960s*. The third source, sponsored content, is a terrific way to get outsiders to provide content for the publication. Anyone who has ever worked for a print publication knows the need to "feed the beast," and the more often a publication appears, the hungrier it is for fresh material. Online publications have a bottomless pit.

HOW PUBLISHERS IMPLEMENT NATIVE ADVERTISING

Now that we've explored the differences, let's look at how various publications handle native advertising to see how that might affect our definition.

Forbes.com typically features five or six "top stories" that are either written by "Forbes staff" or a "contributor" (with a mini-bio on each that links to a longer bio, if you're really interested). The next section features a few video stories, then five "most popular" stories, and then "Forbes Brand*Voice*," which is branded content, in the middle of the opening page of the website. (Below this are many more stories and videos.)

But our interest is the branded content, and one example is an article from "JPMorgan ChaseVoice" entitled "How Can You Balance Work and Life?" If this subject interests you and you click on it to read it, you'll find the writer begins her piece by stating outright (in the very first sentence of the article) that she's "a small business executive at Chase—but that's only a part of who I am."

Again, it's crystal-clear that *this* article is *not* written by the Forbes staff, or even a Forbes contributor; it's written by someone at JPMorgan Chase (or whatever company is providing the sponsored content). One person interviewed for this book summed this up very succinctly: "When something says 'OracleVoice' at the top of the page, people get that it's from Oracle."[19]

And just to make sure, in case it's *not* crystal-clear to readers, there's an explanation immediately following the "Forbes Brand-*Voice*" heading: "Connecting marketers to the Forbes audience," followed by "What is this?" if the reader is still not sure. If you click on that, you'll get a more detailed explanation:

> Forbes Brand*Voice*® allows marketers to connect directly with the Forbes audience by enabling them to create content and participate in the conversation on the Forbes

digital publishing platform. Each Brand*Voice*® is produced by the marketer. More on Brand*Voice* here, or contact us at brandvoice.com.

Opinions expressed by Forbes Brand*Voice*® Contributors are their own.[20]

When asked if BrandVoice is sufficiently distinctive from the rest of the content on Forbes.com, one journalist answered an unequivocal *yes*:

> I've always tried to not underestimate the intelligence of readers. I think that's a much more respectful way to go about doing media: to credit people that they can tell what's marketing and what's journalism. The best breed of advertising gets beyond that paradigm where advertisers are actually doing things that are useful for you, so in some ways it's somewhat immaterial. If they're factually reporting things and doing it in a way that you find useful and it's giving you interesting information, then they're doing a great job with it, and as long as the thing is marked where it comes from, I think people are savvy enough to figure it out. The best native advertising is also doing a really good job of telling you something useful, of doing the job of a journalist, even if the people who are funding it are not journalists. Those are the ones that are really successful."[21]

Here's an example, from Forbes.com (though keep in mind that the problem with citing examples from online publications in a book is the evanescence of the original post):

SAP*Voice:* A Matter of Digital Trust: Understand Your Security Risks and Fix Them Now

Deepak Krishnamurthy, Justin Somaini, and Ryan VanDyk, SAP

It's clear that digital technology offers a unique opportunity to reimagine everything about our world. Smart machines are getting smarter. Billions of people around the world are connected socially, collectively, and digitally. And all of this is **read »**

Forbes has had such success with BrandVoice that it's becoming more candid about the program. In late 2015, Forbes said that approximately 35 percent of its total advertising revenues were generated by its BrandVoice partners (which presumably also includes display advertising revenues from these BrandVoice partners)— which had reached a new high of 100 companies, including SAP (as noted above), Northwestern Mutual, and Mercedes-Benz. It also touted some other numbers:

- Those 100 BrandVoice partners published more than 6,700 posts between 2010 and 2015.
- Those 6,700 posts received more than 55 million page views, again between 2010 and 2015.[22]

Many other publications besides Forbes are featuring native ads, so let's take a look at another online publication: Politico (politico.com), which launched in 2007 and publishes "news and information . . . at the intersection of politics and policy." At the time of this writing, it claims to publish approximately 3,000 stories, 2,000 news alerts for subscribers, and 1,000 morning newsletters in an average month (as well as 30,000 printed copies of its Washington newspaper on 150 print days each year). On a typical day, politico.com features about 20 articles as part of "The Afternoon Report": these articles cover a wide range of what's happening in U.S. politics.[23]

In the middle of all those articles is a piece of sponsored content—which is labeled (you guessed it): "Sponsored Content." All of the site's news articles use headlines in black type against a white background, some with pictures of the subjects of the articles. In contrast, the sponsored content appears in a colored box.

Politico.com has included "sponsored content" from a wide variety of sources, including these:

- "Solving the Career Readiness Crisis," by Chauncey Lennon, JPMorgan Chase

- "Without Action, Alzheimer's Will Overwhelm Federal Budget by 2050," written by the Chief Public Policy Officer of the Alzheimer's Association
- "Electric Co-Op Looks to Carbon Solutions and New Innovations," by the CEO/GM of Basin Electric Power Cooperative
- "Business Leadership on Achieving Climate Goals," by Anne M. Finucane, Vice Chairman, Bank of America
- "The European Commission Could Well Score an Own Goal," by Mark Lichtenhein, Chairman of the Sports Rights Owners Coalition

In addition, when you click on a "sponsored content" article, a blue banner comes up at the top of the new page. On the far right-hand side of that banner appears "What is sponsored content?" for those readers who don't know. If you click on that question, you'll see this answer:

> About POLITICO's Sponsor-Generated Content Program: Sponsor-generated content is content produced or curated by an advertiser that lives on POLITICO and is promoted alongside POLITICO's own editorial content. The content will be identified as "sponsor-generated content" anywhere it may appear on the website. POLITICO's editorial department has no involvement in the creation of this content.[24]

That's crystal clear: the site's editorial department has *no involvement* in the creation of this content. And if that's not clear enough, this little blurb finishes with a call to action for anyone who's interested in writing and publishing their own "sponsor-generated content" on the Politico website: "*Advertisers* interested in sponsor-generated content can learn more here" (emphasis mine).

Other publications indicate their branded content differently. For example, let's look at ELLE.com, the online version of the fashion and lifestyle print magazine (Figure 1.1). When it features native advertising, it will label it with a heading along the lines of "Created by ELLE for _____" (whichever company curated and sponsored that piece).

FIGURE 1.1 ELLE.com branded content for Bulgari

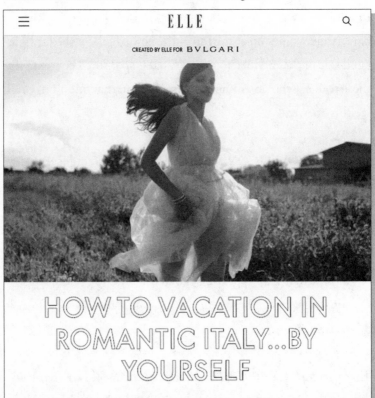

That's also what Cosmopolitan.com does. In the example in Figure 1.2: "16 New Drugstore Beauty Products You'll Be Obsessed With," the content is clearly labeled "Created by Cosmopolitan for Maybelline." This photo gallery recommends 16 new beauty products that can be purchased at a local drugstore. Not all are Maybelline products. The content is interesting and well produced, and I'm confident that readers who are interested in the topic will find the information valuable and helpful.

FIGURE 1.2 Cosmopolitan.com branded content for Maybelline

When asked if there are particular Hearst Magazines websites that feature more native advertising than others, Kate Lewis, SVP,

Editorial Director for Hearst Magazines Digital Media, indicated that it's not so much a brand-to-brand differentiation and that native advertising can "really vary widely" and is "most extensive on the sites where we sell the most ads."

NATIVE ADVERTISING USING VIDEO

As mentioned at the beginning of this chapter, native advertising isn't done only in digital text and photo form; it's also done in video form. For example, Verse is a company that, according to its website, has "assembled a team of experts with deep experience across news, gaming, film and advertising. The resulting platform sets a new standard for artful storytelling that combines emotional impact with measurable and meaningful engagement." This can be seen in a fascinating video story it created about climbing Mount Everest in which it used footage from The North Face, a company that manufactures high-performance apparel, footwear, and equipment for mountain climbers, skiers, and other outdoor enthusiasts. It's a terrific example of native advertising for the company: viewers will want to watch the video because they're interested in the climb, and they won't care that the video was created and/or produced by North Face, because the company isn't doing in-your-face advertising via the video.

Red Bull is another brand that is doing this well. One way the company promoted its energy drinks was via sponsorship of snowboarder Shaun White, a relationship that lasted four years. In one example of native advertising with White, Red Bull built the Olympic athlete a huge half-pipe in the mountains so he could practice for the X Games extreme sports competitions. Red Bull took video footage of White practicing, and the company aired that footage, but nowhere in the video was anything said about the energy drink itself or whether White consumed or didn't consume Red Bull. Instead, the video focused on the *lifestyle* of people like Shaun White: it created an emotional experience around the brand that makes viewers develop an affinity for the brand.

Even better is the fact that this type of advertising is measurable, the same way anything else on the web is: by tracking how many people have watched or clicked on it. One journalist pointed out that it's possible to even purchase products via these ads, although that hasn't been done yet.[25]

A DEFINITION OF NATIVE ADVERTISING

It's time to define native advertising. After considering a wide range of points of view, what have we learned? Several things; including:

- Content marketing and native advertising are different types of programs, and branded content is a form of native advertising.
- The IAB has formally defined native advertising and created six classifications to describe the different types of native advertising.
- The sixth category of native advertising includes branded content as well as sponsored content.

- Native advertising is "an exciting new way for digital marketers to engage with the consumer" and "a new source of advertising revenue for publishers."[26]

All things considered, I believe Sharethrough's definition is the most succinct and all-encompassing: "Native advertising is a form of paid media that follows the form and function of the site or user experience that it lives within."[27] So throughout the rest of this book, we'll bear that definition in mind as we explore the ins and outs of native advertising.

CHAPTER 2

NATIVE ADVERTISING:

WHERE IT BEGAN,

WHERE IT'S GOING

Back in the 1930s and 1940s, radio programs were regularly interrupted to remind listeners who sponsored that lovely music, weepy soap opera, or creepy mystery ("the Shadow knows!") that had listeners on the edge of their seats. Early television featured programs that were clearly funded by their sponsors—for example, *Kraft Television Theatre* and *Texaco Star Theatre*, a comedy-variety show that was originally broadcast on radio from 1938 to 1949 and then on TV from 1948 to 1956. As advertising veteran Steve Piluso said, "[Native advertising] has actually been around for decades. . . . Texaco's brand goals were to be seen as the enabler of the expansion of America through auto travel and the national highway system."

Troy Young, President of Hearst Magazines Digital Media, interviewed for this book, noted that, for a very long time, TV has found interesting ways of bringing brands into a program, whether via sponsorship like the *Subway Postgame Show* or product placement in a dramatic piece of content. Not only that, but brands also use subtler ways to get their products noticed. For example, at the end of many sports events on TV, the winning coach is typically interviewed after the game, and it seems there's always a Gatorade in front of that coach. That's not a coincidence. As this publisher summed up, "TV has been pushing the boundaries between the editorial product and advertising for a long time, and I would argue that the market has held them to a very different standard than print. . . . [In fact] if I put a Gatorade bottle on the cover of a magazine, people would flip, or there would be a lot of discussion from some of the industry bodies around *what is the relationship between editorial and commercial messaging on the cover of a magazine?* I'm just saying that those roles are changing."

Native advertising is often compared to old-fashioned print advertorials—those pages in magazines or newspapers that looked different from the rest of the publication, either because they were set in a different typeface, or because they were enclosed in a box, or, most often, because they included the word "Advertorial" or "Advertisement" at the top of the page (albeit often in very faint or tiny type).

When Ed McLoughlin, then global head of media and data sciences at Hewlett-Packard, was interviewed for this book about the origins of native advertising, he put it this way: "Some level of native advertising has always been around. It just became digital." He pointed out that newspapers and other print media always ran advertorials, and he also talked about television, where "much of the original programming, before the TV spot was standardized, was 100 percent sponsored by an individual brand [such as] Colgate. . . . These techniques have been around in one form or another." The way McLoughlin looks at native advertising, published content that's made to look or feel like branded content can be considered native.

Digital, McLoughlin says, has blurred the distinction more than print, radio, or television did, because native ads now contain links to their content, and, in some cases, their content is designed to trick or prompt a click more than to actually inform the reader, which, in his view, makes the concept a lot more troublesome.

Todd Haskell at Hearst Magazines Digital Media made a similar point about print and digital when he described how he came to Hearst from "an old-line journalism organization" (the *New*

York Times) and mentioned that "organizations have been doing native advertising in one way, shape, or form for 50 years. The *New York Times* has been [publishing] advertorial sections . . . in the newspaper since the 1950s."

Haskell explained that "the big distinction" between native advertising and advertorials "is that advertorials were very clearly kept at a very long arm's length from the actual people who were creating content for the organization every day." In contrast, native advertising is frequently created not only by traditional advertising agencies' creative staffs but also by the publications in which the ads will appear.

That's a good thing, says Haskell: "For most progressive publishing organizations, they've recognized the fact that we actually will do the best possible job, not just for the advertiser, but for the reader, by having our core content creators have some involvement in this, because it just results in content that is . . . actually a good reader experience, because it's created by the people who do this every day, and I think that's the holy grail for both the reader and the advertiser, where we can start making these experiences actually good for the reader."

Adam Kasper also described the similarities between native advertising and advertorials. When he was interviewed for this book, Kasper was the chief media officer for Havas Media North America. Havas's clients have included asset-manager Fidelity Investments, luxury goods giant LVMH (Louis Vuitton Moët Hennessy), and many other notable companies. (Kasper has since taken a position at another company.)

Kasper believes that native advertising is an "evolution" of advertorials, though he points out that with advertorials, "There were very clear church and state lines that every publisher strictly adhered to. You can't have advertising influence editorial, and everyone totally got it, but then the Internet came along, and things changed dramatically, because the lines became blurred."

There's that church-and-state differentiation I talked about in the Introduction. So, how did we get from sponsorships on radio and television and advertorials in newspapers and magazines to digital native advertising, and how did the distinctions between church and state become so blurred?

THE EVOLUTION OF NATIVE ADVERTISING IN DIGITAL PUBLISHING

Perhaps by taking a closer look at "when the Internet came along" and "how native advertising began to take hold among digital publishers," we can find the answer.

Remember the early days of digital? For those of you who don't, here's a quick refresher course. Many consider August 6, 1991, the day the World Wide Web became publicly available,[1] and 1995 is often considered the first year the web became commercialized.[2] It may surprise some of you who weren't around then, but in the early days of the Internet, there was, as one author put it, "a tidal wave of flaming from 'a cyberspace community peopled by academics and intellectuals' who regarded a commercialized Internet as 'advertising hell.'"[3] Eventually, as we all know, the academics and intellectuals lost that battle. The result was the Internet of today with publishers vying for branded content.

This change, however, did not happen overnight. E-mail began in the mid-1990s—AOL, Prodigy, and CompuServe dial-up services all began in 1995—although even then not everyone had a computer on his or her office desk, let alone at home. There were no tablets or smartphones; in fact, flip phones and BlackBerrys were just beginning to take off. The "dot-com" craze of online businesses didn't happen until the late 1990s (around 1997 or so), but people were skittish back then about buying things online, because of the need to give out credit card information, which of course is commonplace today.

Online marketing consisted of a web page, which was usually just a brochure of information about a company. Many businesses hadn't yet registered their brand's domain name and many had not yet adopted interactive websites. Early digital advertising was very primitive, including "pop-up ads"—banners that jumped off of the web page, forcing people to look at them. To understand how intrusive they were, picture someone on the street wearing an old-fashioned "sandwich board" ad; now picture that person running into traffic, in front of your car, forcing you to read what he's advertising: "HUGE GOING-OUT-OF-BUSINESS SALE!!! 50% OFF EVERYTHING!" That's what these banner ads were like. In the words of one person interviewed for this book, "advertising online got really, really invasive and insidious; it got in everybody's face, and people started to really despise it, and that became a real problem for the industry."[4] Today, we have interstitials—an ad inserted before or after the thing being searched for —an evolution of pop-up ads.

However, he went on to defend native advertising: "A good story these days is a good story, and as long as native advertising doesn't pretend to be journalism, there's no reason a brand can't tell a compelling story. Part of what happened to advertising and why it broke down online through the 2000s and 2010s is the creative just got really terrible. Nobody minds a good, funny Budweiser ad on TV, but everyone hates the fiftieth car ad they see with the wet roads. [That type of advertising] just gets in the way. All of the advertising online, or much of it, has become like the bad car ad."[5]

Some savvy marketers started thinking, *What if we try to tell stories in ways that go with the flow of how people actually use the Internet, instead of trying to get in everybody's face and annoy them and attract or divert their attention?* That's where the idea of "native advertising" seemed to originate, because the ads were "going native" with the publications on which they appeared.

Some publications eased into native by hiring—or contracting with—writers and editors to write *generally* about trends in a particular line of business, and a company working in that business would "sponsor" that content (i.e., pay for it) for six months or a year. For example, suppose the topic was logistics: the publication would hire someone to write an article on that topic, and the article would be sponsored by, say, FedEx. The article wouldn't include any information specific to how FedEx conducts business; it would simply describe current shipping trends. The sponsoring company wouldn't have any control over what was written, nor would it be able to review or approve the content. In fact, there was no direct contact between the editorial side and the sponsor. These publications weren't yet offering native advertising, but with this approach to sponsored content, they "flirted with the concept."[6]

Of course, news and business publications weren't the only early adopters of native advertising. As one publisher pointed out, "It's also important to recognize that lifestyle publications, particularly in the fashion space, have had nuanced relationships with fashion companies since the beginning of time; [when they] used clothing in their shoots and [their] editors worked very closely with fashion companies."[7]

Although most people can't pinpoint exactly when native advertising started to appear, most people generally agree that 2010 sounds about right. BuzzFeed was founded in 2006, but it didn't really take off until years later: "BuzzFeed is killing it, and its older rivals are rattled" proclaimed one headline in late 2014.[8]

"I think native advertising, in some ways, has always been there; 'native advertising' as a name is relatively new, but the idea of native advertising is not." That's the view of Felix DiFilippo, publisher and CRO of *Car and Driver* and *Road & Track*, who previously worked for *Forbes*, the *Atlantic*, and *Money* magazine. Musing on it a bit more, he added:

> I think what's really changed is how well publishers can create and execute on native advertising. Over the past few years, publishers have really been able to home in on how best to create content that's consistent with their brands and consistent with why their readers come to their brands.
>
> I don't remember the first [native ad] I saw. It's hard for me to say, because I'm in the business, so I look for it. . . . If I were just a regular consumer of content searching through sites, [I don't know] if it would stand out [or] offend me. I'm just too close to it. . . . I think . . . Forbes has really taken it

to a whole new level, and they were probably one of the first to exploit it and have major success with native advertising. [But it's only been] in the last three or four years that it's really become a big part of their business. Forbes was always a little ahead of the curve and always trying new and different things, so they were dabbling in it [when I worked for them], but I think over the last few years, it's become a major part of their success.

Another former journalist thought native advertising started to "creep in" to publications sometime around 2010, though it was still "on the sidelines" then and was nowhere near as mainstream as it is now. He had worked at Forbes, and said the magazine later brought in new leadership that was open to trying new ways to bring in revenue: "Forbes was "trying to figure out what was new, what was interesting, what could work, what could actually make money." And one of these changes was in the format, from the more traditional website model that the magazine had been using to more of a blog-posting website, "along the lines of the *Huffington Post.*"

This same former journalist said that one business magazine he worked for didn't really do much native advertising at that time—not because it had made a conscious decision not to, but simply because it wasn't as forward-thinking as other publications. In contrast to the publication he worked for, he noted that Forbes seemed to be "more adventurous" and more willing to push the boundaries of advertising, to experiment and try new things. As an ex-journalist, he was perhaps a bit more candid than others, who seemed to be more protective of their employers. In fact, he went so far as to say that one business magazine he worked for "would have been happy to sell just about anything [in terms of advertising] if it was appropriate."

Another journalist summed up companies' need to stay ahead of the curve: "Media needs to constantly evolve and change and experiment and try, and if it doesn't, we're dead meat." He also cited Forbes.com as doing "a great job" with native advertising:

> Forbes had BrandVoice, which Lewis DVorkin and Tim Forbes devised. Their idea was to let brands tell their stories in a transparent way, and let them duke it out for attention along with everybody else. If they tell stories well, if they present meaningful information that's of use to people, and they do it in a way that's compelling, it will help them build their brands. So let them do it, and give them equal footing with everybody else on the Forbes platform. That's what Forbes did, and it was fairly revolutionary.

Jeff Ratner is executive vice president of Zenith/The ROI Agency, a media services agency that has done native advertising work for companies providing financial services, entertainment, and gaming (and others, of course). Ratner views native from an advertiser's perspective and is one of those who thinks that while "native as a term probably became more fashionable [in 2013], creating and embedding content within relevant contextual environments has been around forever [in the form of] advertorials and sponsorships."

In his view, native advertising evolved from sponsorship and dates back to the creation of advertising; only the form has changed. By that he means, "It is more in line with the context of the content it's around, but even more [important, it is aligned with] the . . . characteristics of those consuming the content. Native has gotten smarter over time as [advertisers have] gotten smarter about whom we're targeting our messages to."

DVorkin agrees and describes his reaction as a publisher to these changes: "All of a sudden, marketers were creating content, and [True/Slant] made the site so their content would rise and fall on the merits of how many people read them or watched them; the same on social media, whatever it was. Back then . . . no one was doing what we were doing, except for BuzzFeed, but their [content] was very different. . . . it was entertainment-y. No one called it native advertising back then. As a matter of fact, when I got to Forbes, [the media] actually [said branded advertising was] . . . 'destroying journalism.' All the media. . . . but that's another story."

Meredith Levien, who worked for Forbes for five and a half years as a publisher and then as chief revenue officer, also believes it was Forbes that launched native advertising. "Lewis DVorkin had the idea that consumers, marketers, and journalists would all have the same tools and the same form in which to express themselves in thoroughly labeled ways, so you always knew who was talking. To me, Lewis DVorkin from Forbes (and his original company, True/Slant) and Jonah Peretti from BuzzFeed on the publisher side were the market makers for native advertising and branded content, which is what it morphed into. Twitter and Facebook also were the market makers for it, because the idea was that there was one container of content, and everybody used the same container."

LEWIS DVORKIN AND
FORBES'S PARADIGM SHIFT

Since DVorkin was one of the prime market makers of native advertising on the Internet, it makes sense to take a look at his background and at how Forbes handles native advertising. Lewis DVorkin worked at the *New York Times*, the *Wall Street Journal*, *Newsweek*, and AOL. He started his own company, True/Slant, in 2009, which Forbes initially invested in and then acquired outright in 2011, bringing DVorkin and his team along to lead both editorial and product development at Forbes. Tim Forbes worked very closely with DVorkin to develop these ideas. Tim Forbes, Steve Forbes, and Mike Perlis, CEO of Forbes Media, closely collaborated with DVorkin to develop a new business model at Forbes for both the editorial contributor model and branded content advertising products. Elevation Partners' Roger McNamee and Ted Meisel were also instrumental in this paradigm shift at Forbes. Elevation Partners was a major investor in Forbes Media at the time.

As DVorkin tells it: "It became very clear to me that the economics of journalism were broken, and, in some ways, journalism itself was broken, especially in a world of Internet publishing, when you could see there were so many people out there in the universe who actually knew a lot of things and weren't able to make their way through publishing via traditional media, whether it was newspapers, magazines, books, or whatever they could publish on their own. The future of journalism needed more than just another good story. There needed to be new models—for the newsroom, for labor, [and] for how you pay for content. (At that point, I didn't see a new model for how advertisers pay, but that came . . . a little bit later.) Without new models, nothing was going to change . . . so we set out to create some new models. That was True/Slant."

In running True/Slant and later Forbes product and editorial, DVorkin operates in a different way from how a traditional print editor or publisher does. His title is chief product officer, which encompasses a broad range of responsibilities, including those of editor, publisher, marketer, PR person ("evangelist," in his words), and salesperson/revenue generator. Although some people might think that makes him the proverbial fox in the henhouse, he thinks this new blended, cross-functional approach is necessary. "In the traditional world, media was your editor and your publisher, and they didn't talk; and you [also] had salespeople who didn't talk to editors. And that's not a very good way to run a product in the new world of digital publishing."

Interestingly, when other journalists write about DVorkin, the peg—whether the article is positive or negative—usually revolves around the blurring of the distinction between "church and state"—news and advertising. One intriguing article was titled, "Why are journalists hostile to Lewis DVorkin?" The article explains it's because he's "telling them to get real." The article also calls him "the unstoppable force." But another article says he creates "fake news."[9]

He defended this by explaining the origin of True/Slant: it presented the *contributors'* truth, as they perceived it. As the name indicates, whatever they wrote was their slant on the truth. In addition, the product True/Slant built for marketers was Ad/Slant, which was the *advertisers'* slant on the truth. Therefore, no "fake news" was published by True/Slant; instead, True/Slant presented a perspective either from a contributor with knowledge of his or her subject, or from a marketer with expertise in his or her industry. True/Slant never called it "news"; instead, it was content and insights and information. As DVorkin said, "Not all journalistic insights and information turn out to be accurate. Sometimes not all marketer information turns out to be accurate. That's not a defense. Those are just the realities of the world we live in."

The general public believes that journalists write true and factual information, whereas marketing information is all hype and spin. (There are also many skeptics who don't believe anything they read, but that's another subject for another book.) In reality, however, some journalism is true, and some is spin, and the same can be said about marketing. DVorkin says his goal was "to encourage marketers to create content that was informational in perspective and analysis based on their expertise [that was] insightful, and if the reader wanted it, they'd read it, and if they didn't, [it] wouldn't get any views . . . , the same way if a contributor produced crap, [it] wouldn't get any views either. It seems so quaint today but back then, it seemed like craziness."

Jeff Ratner made a similar point. As he sees it, the lines between content and advertising began to blur almost from the beginning. "I worked on things 20 years ago [around 1996] for AT&T business-to-business services that no one would have called native, when the notion that an advertiser could also be a content producer started bubbling up. We built out a whole content section on Prodigy. This was long, long ago. (Remember, AOL, Prodigy, and CompuServe only began in 1995.) Often in the business-to-business space, you're leveraging content, because . . . a lot of your clients have content and [are interested] in building out information and sponsorships in native environments."

Ratner firmly believes that if the goal of advertising is to provide value, embedding that value in relevant spaces with relevant audiences is where the future of advertising lies. Therefore, he says, "being less disruptive and more informative, creating value for both the advertiser and the consumer is [the direction] we need to head towards, and native placements, focused on seamless integration and content, [will] provide that forum."

He added, at Zenith "our goal is to shamelessly integrate the advertising message with the content around it." Zenith developed two streams. The first was programmatic and audience-based buying, ads delivered based upon who was seeing them—regardless of the context; the second was native, which integrated the message and was contextually relevant to the content around it. Now, Ratner says, those two streams, audience and content, are coming together, and "we are starting to create more effective messages in more relevant places against audiences who are more receptive."

The new world of digital publishing has changed so much regarding the publishing of content and advertising. Troy Young, president of Hearst Magazines Digital Media, thinks that "native advertising is fundamentally about taking friction out of the advertising consumption experience. When you don't have an opportunity to jam advertising down the throat of a consumer, you have to find what's in it for them." In other words, advertisers need to find the age-old *value proposition* for their market, for the consumers they're targeting, which is a good thing. Young's perception is that, for the last five years or so, brands have had to "make content more relevant and interesting by finding connections between where that brand lives and what's important" to readers.

He contrasted this with the way digital advertising used to be done before native came along: "display advertising said, *hey, look over here!*" That approach forced consumers to do two things at once: read content and look at an ad on the side of the page, which was not only intrusive but also not very effective. Or maybe it wasn't effective *because* it was so intrusive? Either way, native advertising eliminated that approach by making ads part of the feed, so that the advertising content fits into its environment, which makes it easier for consumers to consume.

Of course, doing that well is not as easy as it sounds, as Young recognizes. "The hard part with native is really finding the way to a consumer so it's an enjoyable experience."

FOSTERING A MORE ENJOYABLE EXPERIENCE

BuzzFeed and its founder and CEO, Jonah Peretti, are often mentioned as creators of enjoyable branded content, particularly in the entertainment space. Jay Widlitz, cofounder of Brandtale, the largest native advertising database, wholeheartedly agrees: "Buzz-Feed was really the pioneer of [native advertising], and it's done a fantastic job with it." Meredith Levien of the *New York Times* agrees, and she summed up BuzzFeed's success perfectly: "I think BuzzFeed does entertaining branded content extraordinarily well. . . . They're famous for so many pieces, but "Dear Kitten" was to me the best representation of a crushingly good piece of branded content. I thought that was hilariously funny and had value in its own right." I hadn't seen it until Meredith mentioned it, but this video of an older cat educating a new kitten in the household was indeed sweet and clever—and great advertising for Purina's Friskies brand.

Steve Piluso looks at native advertising or branded content "as a Trojan horse strategy to camouflage advertising in a way that feels more like content that is welcomed by readers and viewers [as opposed to overt advertising] that feels intrusive and inauthentic." He continues, "I think the authenticity is really the key to the whole thing." What's more, he believes "you don't have to necessarily deeply camouflage something if the messaging and the brand are authentic to the environment and the viewers' or readers' expectation of [a certain] experience on that platform." He points out that creating this experience is vital even in traditional print advertising. "I spend a lot of my time working on technology accounts," he explains, "and . . . when we look at focus group data from people about their experiences reading these publications, they always say that the ads are part of the [editorial content]."

Thus, it seems that native advertising when it is successful must be entertaining and/or informative; it must be authentic and blend in with the publication; it mustn't shout at or distract the reader; and, perhaps most important, it must meet readers' and viewers' expectations.

That's a pretty tall order. How did advertisers, marketers, and creators respond to those high and difficult-to-meet expectations? Up to this point, we've mostly heard about native advertising from the publishers' perspective. Now let's put the shoe on the other foot and see how some of the early adopters came to native advertising, how they viewed it, and how they implemented it.

Alexa Christon, head of media innovation for General Electric, believes GE was one of the earliest companies doing native advertising since the mid-2000s. By 2010, the company was creating content that appealed to audiences across key programming and cultural moments: GE put an Olympics commentator on video and pushed that across social media; it also worked with NBC and several other partners.

Another early adopter of native advertising was Qualcomm, the $100 billion manufacturer of semiconductor and telecommunications equipment that powers many consumer electronics products used every day. If you're not familiar with Qualcomm, you're not alone: as The Verge succinctly summed up: "Qualcomm is the mobile industry's equivalent of a god: omnipotent and omnipresent, but invisible to the naked eye. The company that was founded on the premise of building 'quality communications' can now be found inside every major smartphone in the U.S." That includes Apple and Samsung phones.

Liya Sharif, Qualcomm's global brand strategy and advertising leader, said that when she came onboard in 2009, content marketing had just started to percolate; it was beginning to be understood as a discipline; and it was just starting to become part of the lexicon.

As Sharif saw it, for native advertising to really work it had to be approached from a journalistic rather than a marketing standpoint, so she applied the rules of traditional journalism to the creation of brand journalism content. The first thing she did was hire a content team, several former journalists to create the branded content she envisioned. She wanted "people on staff that really understood what it [was] to actually fact-check and create stories that break through in a way that news stories would. . . . I hired a person from *USA Today*, a former editor; two people from *PC magazine*—former writers. We also had a couple of writers in-house, but they were more marketing writers. . . . [In this way,] we started to build a team that had [a] mix [of journalists and marketers]. . . . We supplemented [our in-house staff] with a really great agency that was formed back then, called Codeword. . . . They had compiled a whole team of former journalists to [tackle the] dilemma [that] branded [content precipitated. At the time,] there weren't enough people who understood how to write and create this type of content. Both the staff reporters and journalists at Codeword had a deep understanding of technology, so they were able to hit the ground running and started to churn out this new type of content."

Not long after she hired the team, around 2010 or 2011, Qualcomm launched a website, internally known as the "Branded Journalism" site—its real name was Spark. It was then that it really started creating and promoting branded journalistic content. Spark was almost a separate entity; it wasn't really branded as Qualcomm. Sharif explained, "[We] started producing journalistic content, and . . . distributing it throughout the web through native advertising. [It was] the best way to start experimenting with native advertising. . . . [Qualcomm] has been doing that for several years, and we've learned a lot of lessons [including] that we definitely needed larger budgets for native advertising to bring people to the site. [Native advertising] became part of the mainstream [but] Qualcomm [was] there [in] the very, very early days; trying to understand it, trying to figure out what worked."

According to global content and media strategist Luke Kintigh, Intel dipped its toe in the native advertising water sometime around 2012 or '13. It had a two-pronged approach. Like Qualcomm that had its own digital magazine, Intel had an online media property called IQ (IQ.intel.com) which was, he says, its "attempt at being more like *Wired* and less like a corporate website. . . . We really tried to embrace the brand as a publisher [would, and, as a result] we have a property that's generating a lot of content [and] that [works] well [as] native advertising."

Originally, Intel used native advertising to amplify its content on IQ as well as all the native feeds and the news platforms; the company also worked directly with publishers to co-create content for specific programs and campaigns. "Over the last two or three years, we've moved a lot closer to really amplifying our own content [on] IQ. . . . We still do co-created content, but we don't do nearly as much as we did two or three years ago."

CASE STUDY: THE *NEW YORK TIMES*

When the *New York Times* set about launching its T Brand Studio offering native advertising and branded content, it faced an interesting and somewhat daunting challenge. How it went about meeting that goal provides an interesting case study.

"The *Times* as a brand overall in the world is differentiated for the quality and breadth and depth of our content, also for our product experience and our user experience digitally, and the combination of those things means we make something that's worth paying for," explained Meredith Levien, who came to the *Times* originally to run advertising and now is responsible for all of the *Times* revenue—consumer, video, subscription, and advertising. Levien knows what she's talking about—she launched T Brand Studio.

She joined the *Times* in July 2013, and she and her team launched T Brand Studio in January 2014. As she described, it had zero revenue in 2013. It grew to between $10 million and $20 million in revenue in 2014, and more than doubled in 2015. Levien says they expected to grow at a similar rate in 2016. How did they do it? That brings us back to where we started: the *Times* brand. Levien knew they had to do it in a way that would "at minimum aspire to live up to the quality standard of the *New York Times*, [which meant they had] to tell really, really high-quality stories." So rather than use a network of freelancers or one of the many creator networks, they decided to hire their own people.

Today, T Brand Studio is basically a commercial content operation that employs journalists, developers, creative technologists, visual designers, photographers, videographers, filmmakers, and people with a deep background in marketing—about 100 people—mostly content providers, all of whom work in all parts of the branded content supply chain. Levien says its role is to "help brands do four things: develop content strategy, create content, distribute content, and measure the impact of that content."

The decision to key their eye on quality and do it all in-house seems to be paying off. According to Levien, we have "100 really high-quality makers working in T Brand Studio, and because [we are] the *Times*, we can attract extraordinary talent.

We've definitely been lauded for the quality and the depth of our creative work." In addition, she thinks they are really good at strategy, figuring out the story they should tell, and, she says, in the last six to 10 months, they have also gotten really good at distribution, which now allows them to charge for branded content on a cost-per-view model, "and if [we] deliver those views efficiently [because] the quality of the content is so good that people organically want to engage with it, [we and the marketer do well]."

At the time Levien was interviewed in spring 2016, T Brand Studio had completed approximately 150 productions. Its first piece of content was an 800-word piece of text accompanied by a picture; its 100th piece of branded content was a virtual reality film for GE, "How Nature Is Inspiring Our Industrial Future," about biomimicry. Says Levien, "We're now doing an extraordinary amount of video, multimedia, and really sophisticated applications of advanced storytelling technology.

"Creative-wise, we've just gotten so much more sophisticated. I think that's actually where we are most differentiated, but we're also really good at content strategy. In the past, a client would come to us [with a] general idea. . . . Sometimes they [would] come to us with a piece of content and all they wanted was distribution or for us to set that content into a context. . . . Today, where we're seeing a lot of the demand for our work is actually building a content strategy. . . . We embed a team of journalists and makers with a client to figure out . . . what the best story or the best series of stories [is] and the best way to tell them."

At the time of the interview, the *Times* had more than 2 million paying subscribers, and it had just crossed the line where it had more paid digital subscribers than print subscribers. Levien explained, "That's not because print is dropping precipitously. It's still a very big and healthy consumer business for us, so we have this very high bar."

There's a lesson here for those who heed it: not all publishers can be the *Times*, but they can offer consistent quality and seamless integration of audience and context.

Todd Haskell at Hearst also attributes online success to quality: "What we've seen is that when our editors ensure the quality of our [online] branded content experience, [the result] is often [among] our best-performing content across every category, not just branded. Literally on some of our sites, the top-performing story of the year was something that we created for an advertiser. So, now what we're trying to do is take that approach and work backwards and apply that same discipline to our printed products. . . . What we're literally doing is [taking an] innovation that started in digital [and applying it] to the legacy products."

THE NEXT BIG THING IN NATIVE ADVERTISING

What's the next big thing in native advertising? We all know the digital world is changing. Just as consumers migrated from desktops to laptops to tablets and smartphones—all of which changed the way they worked, played, banked, shopped, and socialized—so, too, have the ways marketers connected with them.

Many of those interviewed for this book agree with Dhawal Mujumdar, cofounder of software developer AdsNative, who said it this way: "My strong opinion on native advertising [is that] it's the format for the mobile piece—for smartphones—because . . . display ads don't really work well on smartphones." He points to the very real limitations of smartphones: for example, the real estate, meaning the size of the screen and the fact that most display ads require Flash, which doesn't work well on the mobile screen. It comes down to the format, and if native advertising can find the right way to adapt to that context and the audience, smartphones might well be where native advertising is headed.

Heather Dumford, global marketing director of media, ConAgra Foods, agrees that mobile has its limitations when it comes to conventional ad formats, and reports that the company has "strategically moved away from the small banner ads that have traditionally shown up in mobile advertising to more native units. We find that banner ads in mobile are very challenging. Consumers don't love them. For us, they don't perform very well, so we shifted that strategy as well."

"I think app experiences are the best, so I would guess that branded content in an app would perform just as well or better, because it's usually a more natural experience than the web, but I have no data to prove that; that's just my guess," said Ben Darr, cofounder of Brandtale, and then added, "so much traffic is coming on mobile that [we] really need to be building experiences that are amazing for mobile, and also good for [bigger screens].

"We've seen a big shift in the last six months. . . . [B]rands are asking for really good experiences on mobile, and publishers are really spearheading [the effort to find what that is and . . . to deliver it], because that's how they're going to get repeat business now." It makes sense based on the numbers. He pointed out that 60 percent—it can be as high as 70 percent and as low as 50 percent depending on the demographic—of most publishers' traffic comes in on mobile. Therefore, they would want the majority of their users to get the best possible experience, and brand content publishers are starting to get smart about that.

Right now, some people are concerned about the potential for abuse in the mobile area. As Ed McLoughlin pointed out, "You're looking at a mobile screen, there's a lot of content that comes into your news feed that isn't clearly labeled as brand content." On the other hand, he says, "I think that's where you will see a proliferation of native."

According to a 2015 Pew Research survey of smartphone use, "Nearly two-thirds of Americans are now smartphone owners, and for many, these devices are a key entry point to the online world. . . . And for a number of Americans, smartphones serve as an essential connection to the broader world of online information." Pew reports that in 2014:

- 62 percent of smartphone owners used their phone to look up information about a health condition.
- 57 percent used their phone to do online banking.
- 44 percent used their phone to look up real estate listings or other information about a place to live.
- 43 percent to look up information about a job.
- 40 percent to look up government services or information.
- 30 percent to take a class or get educational content.
- 18 percent to submit a job application.[10]

Mujumdar of AdsNative also pointed out that most Facebook and Twitter usage is on smartphones; he estimates 60 percent to 70 percent of the smartphone users access them through their apps or their websites. Mujumdar, who is in his late twenties, believes that the younger generation—by which he means teenagers, who, he says, spend almost 90 percent of their time on their smartphones—will be the "native" generation. Today, he says, they are looking at Snapchat. "They are accessing the same content as we do, but we visit Forbes.com or BuzzFeed.com, they're getting the same content (they are reading longer-form articles), but with a Snapchat app."

And what comes after mobile? Probably something we haven't yet seen, but you can be sure there will be something new. We will explore when native advertising is okay and when native advertising is not okay in the next chapter.

CHAPTER 3

WHEN IS NATIVE

ADVERTISING OK,

AND WHEN IS IT NOT OK?

Native advertising may have started on digital publications like Forbes and BuzzFeed, but it is now ubiquitous, a natural outgrowth of reading information and viewing and interacting with entertainment online. As noted in Chapter 2, to capture readers' attention, native advertising has become a necessity, since display advertising is proving less effective and ad-blocking technology is rapidly being adopted.

As a result, you can find native advertising not only on Buzz-Feed but on just about any online publication you read, from women's magazines like *Cosmopolitan* and *ELLE* to men's magazines like *Esquire*, and business magazines and newspapers including *Forbes* and the *New York Times*. For example, Hearst features native advertising in all 21 of its online magazine publications in the United States (and there are hundreds more internationally, just from Hearst, not to mention all the other magazine publishers.)

Some of these online magazines lend themselves to native advertising better than others. For example, there's more branded content and native advertising on Cosmopolitan.com than on CarandDriver.com. However, that's not a function of the audience or the brand, but of the publishing platform, according to Todd Haskell at Hearst Magazines Digital Media. "We have 19 brands that all operate on a single unified publishing platform. That platform was designed with branded content in mind . . . [however,] I could point to examples on *Road & Track*, [*Car and Driver's*] sister property, that absolutely demonstrate that endemic [well-known] car brands can totally play in this space."

Both of these car magazines feature reviews of cars, but they are never sponsored, because the reviews wouldn't be objective.

(Chapter 4 addresses this in more detail, in the discussion of disclosure guidelines.)

WHAT'S OK?

As mentioned, lifestyle consumer magazines are not the only publications that are featuring native advertising. Hard news publications, including newspapers, are also doing it, though not without some controversy. Veteran journalist and author Michael Wolff pulled no punches when articulating his view on native advertising in a column he wrote for the U.S. digital edition of the *[UK] Guardian*. Wolff described how there was a "historic distinction in publishing" where readers could easily discern "mass from class, the vulgar from the refined." But with the rise of digital journalism and the success of sites like BuzzFeed, even a newspaper as venerable as the *New York Times* "finds itself, grimly, and with the greatest self-pity, having to accept native advertising."[1]

Blogger and author Andrew Sullivan commented in an equally colorful way. When asked whether journalists should lend their editorial expertise to branded content, he exclaimed, "That's not journalism, that's copywriting. It's advertising! To say that no journalist can finance his or her work through readers paying for it is an astonishing indictment of journalism and a lack of confidence in the whole enterprise."

Sullivan went on to say that publications shouldn't *have* to do native advertising: "If you're good enough, you should be able to have your readers subscribe to your site. . . . What does it tell you that BuzzFeed wouldn't even dream of asking its readers to subscribe? Daily Beast can't ask its readership to contribute . . . Gawker [wasn't able to] get people to pay for its product. I don't know why they're not embarrassed that they can't get their readers to support their work." Finally, he condemns publications that feature sponsored content from brands: "The *Guardian* [is] basically deciding to merge with Unilever. They have a whole staff of journalists writing articles with Unilever's funding. It's not journalism, it's public relations."[2]

Not everyone agrees with Wolff and Sullivan.

Linda Miller, director of network journalism and inclusion at American Public Media and a board member at Journalism That Matters, believes that businesses need to communicate with their customers and the public, and that there is a whole range of ways to think about the way they communicate. That includes persuasive advertising (promoting a product) and branded content (providing advice and information, which may not be directly related to the product they're selling, but is aimed at creating a bond with their customers).

In Miller's view, the business of communication is what journalism is all about, and for journalists to erect an iron curtain between writing that's done for a publisher who is, in theory, only interested in the public good, and writing for an advertiser, who has an economic interest in getting the reader to buy something or use a service, seems both unrealistic and ineffective.

She argues that brands always had to communicate with their public; and that, in the old days, they had to go through a media organization. That was because of the narrowness of the pipes available to them, but that is no longer the case because the technology has changed. Today, they are going directly to their audience and, therefore, it makes sense for people in the journalism world to figure out how to assist them with that in some meaningful way."[3]

Bill Densmore, a journalist and principal of Densmore Associates (a firm that includes journalism consultants and researchers) agrees with Miller, "It's a burning issue that journalism, writ large, needs to be addressing in a creative and thoughtful way."

There are others whose view falls somewhere between Wolff and Sullivan and Miller and Densmore. Adam Kasper is one of those who has his doubts but still finds the concept interesting and potentially valuable if done openly. "My belief is that if you're being paid to put a product in your publication, in your content, you should say that. . . . [T]here are too many gray areas."

On the other hand, Kasper thinks that the native industry is interesting because it is very content driven, and because it may be the only technology-led area of the business that is all about content.

WHAT'S *NOT* OK?

Clearly then, the challenge to native advertising is to make it subtle enough that it truly becomes "native"—that it blends in with the surrounding editorial material so that readers will read it and not care that it was written by an advertiser rather than by a journalist or by a journalist on behalf of an advertiser—while at the same time, being sufficiently aboveboard—by clearly identifying the sponsor—that the piece doesn't confuse or irritate readers who may feel that they've been duped into reading something that isn't truly informative but just turns out to be a pitch for some product or company.

So what's *not* OK? Several people interviewed for this book cited the *Atlantic* magazine's "article" on Scientology, which briefly appeared on the magazine's website on Monday, January 14, 2013—and was taken down by the magazine 12 hours later. Entitled "David Miscavige Leads Scientology to Milestone Year," this piece described how Miscavige, the "ecclesiastical leader of the Scientology religion" had led the church in a "milestone" year in 2012, "with the religion expanding to more than 10,000 Churches, Missions and affiliated groups, spanning 167 nations— figures that represent a growth rate 20 times that of a decade ago." Most of the seven-page "article" was then devoted to pictures and brief descriptions of the 12 "Ideal Scientology Churches" that Miscavige opened in 2012 (in the United States, Europe, and Israel).

The piece was labeled "Sponsor Content," highlighted in yellow, with a "What's This?" link next to it, which serves as the disclaimer explaining that:

> This content is made possible by our Sponsor; it is not written by and does not necessarily reflect the views of the *Atlantic*'s editorial staff. See our Advertising guidelines, or email advertising@theatlantic.com to learn more.[4]

However, the hue and cry that rose up when this piece appeared was *not* because the *Atlantic* had included what we now know as branded content or sponsored content or native advertising. Instead, readers were upset because *this particular sponsored content* just didn't belong in the magazine at all. It had nothing to do with the readership or the magazine's usual content.

Within hours, Gawker.com posted this scathing piece, criticizing the magazine's decision to publish the sponsored content:

The *Atlantic* Is Now Publishing Bizarre, Blatant Scientology Propaganda as "Sponsored Content"

Gawker described the *Atlantic*'s article as "an example of the kind of advertising many publishers are turning to as display ad revenue stagnates" and concluded with the sarcastic comment that this was "a bold, proud day for the *Atlantic* and its fine history of journalistic excellence."[5]

Gawker wasn't the only publication to take note of the magazine's error in judgment. No less than the *Washington Post* described the piece as an "advertorial" that "took a rough ride on the Internet yesterday and is now gone from the *Atlantic*'s site."[6] The newspaper also added interesting "facts about the imbroglio," including that native advertising is critical to the *Atlantic*'s livelihood; that digital advertising contributed 59 percent to the overall advertising revenue for the magazine in 2012; but that it wasn't clear how much of that revenue came from native advertising.[7]

As mentioned, the brouhaha caused the magazine to take down the Scientology piece a mere 12 hours after it appeared on the site. Moreover, the *Atlantic* published an official statement about the debacle:

We screwed up. . . . We now realize that as we explored new forms of digital advertising, we failed to update the policies that must govern the decisions we make along the way. . . . We are sorry, and we're working very hard to put things right.[8]

Felix DiFilippo at Hearst was one of several who cited the Scientology article as a native advertising "debacle." In general, DiFilippo believes that native advertising works for all brands and in all publications but "it needs to be done right and be on message on brand. It can't seem forced." He agreed with the general public that the Scientology "article" just didn't fit in with the editorial direction of the *Atlantic*, which is why there was such a backlash against it and why it changed the way the *Atlantic* approaches native advertising as a whole. Indeed, after pulling that piece, the *Atlantic* developed its own native advertising guidelines (which I'll cover in more detail in Chapter 4).

DiFilippo also cited an example of native advertising that he thinks was handled really well. It appeared several years ago in *Sports Illustrated*. It was a sponsored piece for a financial retirement company, and it focused on what various professional athletes were doing since they retired. This piece made sense as a sponsored post because there was "genuine interest" among readers to learn what their heroes were doing, so this type of native advertising worked. Even more interesting is the fact that this sponsored piece appeared in the *print* magazine, long before digital.

Another good example of native advertising cited was an ad for Advil that appeared in *Bicycling* magazine. Steve Piluso mentioned this ad because it "was specifically written for people who experience pain from cycling . . . and was really well suited to the environment." He went on to say that "the problem [with some native advertising] is often you have categories and brands that aren't necessarily welcome in certain environments or don't necessarily make sense in certain environments, and they try to camouflage their message into something else, and that's where it gets a little bit disingenuous for brands."

Many people interviewed for this book cited one particular piece of native advertising that stood out in their minds as an exceptional example. It was an interactive piece on the *New York Times* online site, combining both print and video interviews, about women in the U.S. prison system. Entitled "Women Inmates: Why the Male Model Doesn't Work," it described how the policies and programs of most prisons don't really meet the needs of female inmates. Steve Piluso was the first person who called my attention to this article: he cited it as "one of the gold standards . . . [that] stunned everybody, because it was so brilliant."

He went on to describe it as "a really smart investigative piece" that only became apparent that it was native advertising at the end of the article, when it revealed that it was brought to fruition by *Orange Is the New Black*, the Netflix TV show about women in prison. Piluso—and many others interviewed for this book— cited this piece as an outstanding example because the article was well researched and well written, in keeping with the *Times'* editorial standards, but also because of the close synergy between the topic and the sponsor.

It was called "awesome and elegant" by contently.com, a content marketing platform, which also called attention to the fact that it was "a piece of branded content."[9] Also noted is the fact that there were only a few clues to the link between the *Times* piece and Netflix. One was a tiny banner at the top that indicated "Paid Post" and "Netflix." The second was a brief mention in the article itself—the only mention, in fact—that quoted the author of the book on which the show is based. And the last was a longer banner at the bottom that revealed the connection to the TV show.

Steve Piluso attributed the success of this example of native advertising to the fact that it was written by a journalist at the *Times* who works in a completely dedicated, separate editorial department devoted to writing this type of material. The group consists of true journalists—that is, they are just as skilled, talented, and experienced as any other journalist who writes articles for any other section of the *Times*. Piluso felt this piece had obviously been researched really well, it was chock-full of facts about women inmates, it had (almost) no mention of the TV show that ultimately was revealed as the sponsor, and it was just so well written that it fit in perfectly with the rest of the content on the *Times* site. In other words, it was truly native—which is the goal of every piece of native advertising: to blend in completely with the surrounding content. According to Kissmetrics, "Netflix put their resources towards getting an intriguing piece of content in front of the eyes of over 1 million *New York Times* readers; content that may inspire many of those readers to watch the related Netflix series."[10]

How the piece came about is also interesting. Netflix wanted to do something different to promote *Orange Is the New Black*, and someone on the advertising team came up with the idea to write a piece about how the penal system seems inherently unfair to women. In other words, the idea didn't originate from someone thinking, *how do we sell something for this advertiser?* but from, *how do I tell a really interesting story that should be told to the* New York Times *audience?*

That goal and the fact that the article was written by a true journalist, not an advertising copywriter, are what made this piece of native advertising so memorable and such a great example of truly native advertising. As Piluso so aptly described it: "When you think about the authenticity of these [pieces, you realize] they have to be created not by knockoff writers or knockoff designers; they have to be done by people who would do it anyway if it wasn't brand sponsored. When I got to the end of the piece, I thought, *Wow, that was really smart. That was really interesting.* It really got my attention." He had seen and enjoyed the TV show, but this article made him think about it in an entirely new way. This article—this *ad for a TV show*—was so well written and so informative that when he finished reading it, he thought, *Wow, thank you,* Orange Is the New Black. *You brought me something valuable. I learned something today.*

T Brand Studio, which I discussed in Chapter 2, is the division of the *New York Times* that houses the journalists who create branded content. Meredith Levien, EVP and chief revenue officer at the *Times*, provided further insight into how the "Women Inmates" article came to fruition. She confirmed that it was indeed Netflix that wanted to create some branded content, but it was the *Times* T Brand Studio—the native advertising specialists—who brought depth to the piece. "When our team and T Brand Studio went out to begin reporting on it, to interview psychologists, sociologists, women prisoners, and people who had been in prison and had been released, we realized there was this much richer, deeper, and more journalistic story there about nearly a million women living in incarceration designed for men." Netflix agreed, and that's how the piece developed.

You may recall the discussion in Chapter 2 about Forbes's BrandVoice, which, like T Brand Studio, is exclusively devoted to native advertising. Although it operates differently, Lewis DVorkin at Forbes Media says, they "are the only ones that I'm aware of where the marketer uses the same content management system and publishing tools as our journalists use. It all funnels into the content management system, so everything is created equal. It's distributed equally . . . organically across the site. It always [identifies the writer as a] 'staffer' or 'contributor' and [includes the label] 'BrandVoice.'" DVorkin emphasized that regardless of who wrote the article, it goes through the same content management system. He also emphasized that, unlike Forbes, other publishers don't give marketers access to the same tools they give to journalists and that the Forbes' concept is "one page for everybody, transparently labeled, using the same publishing tools, the same content management system."

One ex-journalist summed up the importance of the writer's credentials to native advertising this way: "[If] you don't really know who [is] blogging . . . if you don't have editorial control over that, if you don't have a process in place and policies in place that actually determine who is writing the articles, and you let anybody do it, then it could just as well be [written by] a marketer or a scam artist, as [by] a bona fide journalist."[11]

WHAT *NOT* TO DO

Of course, not all of the *Times* native advertising is as terrific as the *Orange Is the New Black* piece was. There are also "some really horrible examples," as one person interviewed for this book described an article that was ostensibly on the benefits of fossil fuels and green energy that was labeled "brought to you by BP." Unfortunately, he felt the article "was total nonsense" and an effort by BP "to clean up its image after sullying the entire Gulf and damaging the Caribbean for generations. That was a really bad example, because it didn't ring true. You could see right away that BP was trying to pull the wool over readers' eyes, trying to convince readers that they are actually actively cleaning the environment and looking out for the environment, but I don't think anybody believes that for a second, so it was a bit of a disaster piece."

That article was a particularly egregious example of what *not* to do. Unfortunately, I also heard this:

> The vast majority of what I see is awful. So many marketers are trying so hard to create a different conversation with consumers and to get away from the clutter of basic advertising that they're doing really desperate things to attract audiences. A lot of brands are probably doing more to alienate audiences than galvanize them. If [native advertising] isn't done really, really well and you're a little bit lucky, it's really disingenuous and almost insulting to audiences.

Another example of that came from someone just getting her journalism degree. When asked about the first piece of native advertising she recalled seeing, she cited two pieces—one that she thought was awful; the other she thought was great. "I came across an [article about] Venus, the razor, touting it as 'the best new razor,' and then, all of a sudden, I realized that it was an advertorial." She was no longer interested in the product.

The one she thought was effective was for a shake mix she first became aware of through a native ad that appeared in *Women's Health* magazine, which said that Vega "was the best shake mix for overall health and well-being. [It] was a pretty seamless integration, and I thought, okay, *I'll try it* . . . and that's how I purchased it, so that [ad] was effective."

FINDING A NATURAL FIT

DVorkin points to Facebook as an example of a publisher that has executed well. The regular feed has matured, he says, and seamlessly blends into the content. By ensuring that there is proper disclosure, Facebook users can choose to engage with it or not, "which is much, much better than being hit with a full-page interstitial ad over which the user has no control."

But it's not just that some attempts at native advertising are too obviously ads that make them not work. Sometimes it's bad placement. The worst examples, according to Steve Piluso, are pieces that "force-fit brands into areas where they don't necessarily belong." Sometimes it's low production values; but most often it's the lack of authenticity that causes a native ad to fail.

In contrast, Piluso says, "The best native advertising and brand content has almost zero mention of the brand within the content. . . . It's about understanding what I call *brand permission*. Where does the brand really have permission to play? Where does it naturally fit vs. where is it unwelcome?" Once again, this points to the importance of authenticity. Where does the brand really feel it would be a natural and welcome element; where does the brand really not belong, where does it feel weird? If people feel like they're being overtly sold to after the experience or feel they haven't gotten something of value—something that makes them feel like the brand was a bit altruistic—then it turns people off.

From the audience's point of view, if it's near and dear to what they're thinking about at that moment and relevant to why they're there in the first place, they're going to pay attention to the ad. If they know it's marketing, but feel its relevance right away, then they're going to read it anyway. On the other hand, Piluso thinks a lot of ads aren't really seen, which naturally defeats their purpose. Consumers are smart, and their ability to detect the real from the spurious has become really refined over the past few years. People are skipping over advertising—over stuff that they see no value in—at lightning speed.

Piluso puts it this way, "Now that people have the ability to just filter everything out, they're making those decisions very quickly, so naturally [that] has caused people to better refine their BS meters. If a brand is trying to fool them, it's insulting, and it's probably going to create a pretty negative brand impression."

Satish Polisetti, CEO and cofounder of software developer AdsNative, pointed out ads succeed precisely because they're subtle and don't seem to be selling something. "If you look at a company like GE or Intel, when they go native . . . they produce . . . these amusing videos and articles . . . their expectation is not that we will go and buy [a product] . . . or [apply for] an internship. They are trying to say, "Hey, [we are] GE, [we are] Intel and [we] are as cool as Facebook and Uber for the next engineer . . . coming out of UC Berkeley."

Piluso perfectly summed up native advertising at its best:

I love the idea of content marketing. I think the word I use a lot is *camouflage*, and you shouldn't need to camouflage something if it's really authentic and meaningful to audiences. *Orange Is the New Black* is a perfect example. You didn't need to camouflage the brand within that content. It was great content . . . brought to you by a brand that . . . [was flawlessly] aligned with the editorial platform.

Branded content and native advertising are new forms of advertising, and consumers, marketers, and publishers are observing both effective and ineffective implementations. In the next chapter, we will cover the important topic of native advertising disclosure.

CHAPTER 4

THE ESSENTIALS YOU NEED TO KNOW ABOUT NATIVE ADVERTISING DISCLOSURES, REGULATORY COMPLIANCE, AND POTENTIAL LEGAL ISSUES

As mentioned in the Introduction, there used to be a clear "church/state" separation between a publication's editorial content and its advertising, both in the way the content and advertising were presented and in how the publisher's editorial and advertising staff interacted and functioned. The editorial and ad sales departments were on separate floors; they were never in the same meetings; editors and ad salespeople didn't even talk to each other. There was an invisible but obvious line between them—a line that neither would cross, and if someone did, that someone was almost certainly fired.

Elizabeth Hansen, a recent journalism graduate, thinks that the issue of labeling articles or content as native advertising derives from a generally accepted journalistic code that is meant to keep journalism "transparent, even independent." With some branded content, Hansen says, "even if the [ads are] not labeled as such, you can tell," but with others, you can't always tell until you're halfway through. From her perspective, regulators would not object to native advertising if the articles were clearly labeled to avoid any possibility of deceiving the reader.[1]

Rebecca Babcock, working as a consultant for eBay as senior program manager, Premium Content Partnerships & Communities, recalled the first time she recognized native advertising. "It was probably on Facebook. [I don't remember that it was advertising,] I just remember feeling, *oh, this feels icky,* and . . . as a marketer, thinking . . . that's what we have to do. We have to alert readers that what they're reading is not editorial content. In a way, I almost appreciated that, because it kept the lines very clean and clear, and I remember thinking in digital, *oh, this is going to be interesting. This is a very blurred line, and it's either going to be really cool, or it's going to feel forced."*

The wall between church and state still exists. For example, companies that want to publish an article on Forbes Brand-*Voice* can't ask Forbes journalists to write those articles, or even to help them write those articles. That's simply not allowed, as Lewis DVorkin confirmed: "We have 1,800 contributors who work for Forbes editorial. If you're one of those 1,800 and you want to go work for a BrandVoice company, you can do that, but you can no longer [be a Forbes contributor]. You cannot be part of our journalistic newsroom and work for a BrandVoice partner. You've got to be on one side or the other. You can't do both simultaneously."

HOW PUBLISHERS DISTINGUISH SPONSORED CONTENT

Another practice that has not yet been standardized across the industry is the way in which different publications distinguish sponsored content from journalistic content. If you've read this far, it should be obvious to you that not all publications indicate sponsored content in the same way. For example, ELLE.com's branded content (mentioned in Chapter 1) features the name of the magazine along with the name of the advertiser sponsoring the piece, with the disclosure "Created by ELLE for Bvlgari."

Other commonly used descriptors at different publishers include:

- Advertisement
- Ad
- Promoted
- Sponsored
- Featured partner
- Suggested post[2]

These are often followed by the name of the advertiser's brand: for example, "Presented by [brand]."

While not endorsing specific language, an IAB whitepaper pointed out that "in addition to language, shading, or other visual cues associated with native ads, many publishers also include additional disclosure cues such as a separate roll-over link using language such as "What's this?" . . . [that] makes it clear that the ad content did not come from the publisher's editorial staff and may also include a statement such as 'the content may not necessarily reflect the opinions of the editorial staff.' "[3]

Kate Lewis recognizes that native advertising must be clearly labeled. As Lewis put it:

> I think our audience knows, and they're pretty wise to it. I think
> they can see [the difference between articles] that are sponsored
> and that aren't. My job is to tell a great or useful or emotional
> or meaningful story for my audience . . . my number one goal
> is audience engagement, entertainment, and happiness.

Lewis also points out that in articles of sponsored content, not all of the products are specific to the sponsoring company. For example, the content that appeared on Cosmopolitan.com that offered drugstore beauty product recommendations (described in Chapter 1) did *not* exclusively feature Maybelline products. That diversity of products forestalls readers from complaining that the content is simply a pitch for one company's products. Lewis emphasized that the branded content team decides which products work into a particular story, ensure that they come from a variety of companies, and see that those products are tested before they're endorsed in any native advertising piece.

In her current position at Hearst, Lewis isn't in a direct line for feedback from readers. Each site's editor is more in line than she is to receive that commentary. However, in a former position for another "very communicative" site at another company, she did see a lot of reader feedback. She commented that the feedback was very positive—in fact, she described it as "gratitude for the transparency." Readers of that site understood that some company had paid the site to pitch its products, but because the site was clear and upfront about that, readers were fine with it. Transparency is really all any reader wants, as she reiterated: "That is our obligation as publishers. We need to make it clear that we're in cahoots with someone on this content. We're still going to make it the best it can be, but we have to be clear about the business relationship up front."

Troy Young, President of Hearst Magazines Digital Media, also confirmed that all native ads in Hearst magazines are clearly marked: "In all cases, we're entirely transparent about the relationship between us and the advertiser."

As if to prove Lewis's point, one young journalist interviewed for this book mentioned that she distinctly remembers the first native advertising piece she read because it irritated her so much when she realized that it *was* just a pitch for one particular retailer.

She was reading a listicle (as its name implies, an article in the form of a list) on BuzzFeed.com and she "quit reading halfway through" because every point concluded with "and you can buy this at _____." (I'm not going to name the retailer; the guilty shall remain anonymous.)

Rebecca Babcock at eBay thinks the best native advertising is when it feels organic and natural. For this reason, she says eBay doesn't tell its partners what to write about; instead it encourages them to write about what *their* audience is interested in. "To me, that's as 'organic' as you can get, and Thrillist [a digital men's lifestyle brand], for example, absolutely denotes that it's sponsored, as they should, but if a partner's doing a good job and they're writing great content, what we call great shopping content, it really shouldn't matter if it's sponsored or not."

Advertisers' view of disclosure is a little different from that of publishers. Luke Kintigh of Intel described his experiences with different publishers and how they handle disclosure. "With BuzzFeed, it's 'Intel Presents,' and it's got the logo right upfront of the post.

"With the new platforms that we work with, the Outbrain's, the Sharethrough's, the Taboola's, it's usually in the widgets or in the in-feed native. It's usually a different shade.

"We were the second advertiser to work with the *New York Times* . . . where it's [the opposite of BuzzFeed] and very overkill . . . there is a separate site that has a big blue box around it. [At the *Times*] It was 'Sponsored by Intel.' [The] consumer was [always] getting the message that Intel was behind the content."

Meredith Levien of the *Times* describes their system this way: "There's a carousel in the middle of our homepage, a block of stories that says 'from our advertisers,' and those are all branded content productions. . . . We've got paid posts running every day, and you can always find the carousel on our homepage. You can also find [promotions throughout] . . . depending on who they're targeting . . . always very labeled . . . because we never want to trick our readers into thinking this is *New York Times* journalism."

When Intel promotes "earned media" (unpaid positive publicity) as opposed to product or brand promotions, it gets the word out by promoting it on a native advertising platform, but the source would be the magazine or website that published the article or review. Then, Kintigh explains, it is "promoted by Intel, so there's a couple of caveats on how exactly the different . . . publishers present it." He adds, "The days are coming when there's going to be a lot more consistency they have to disclose."

"You have to be transparent about who's communicating that message in native advertising," asserts Hilary Batsel, Microsoft's Marcom media director, consumer brands. "So if I'm a consumer and I'm on Yahoo, [for example] and there's a paid video. If it is not clearly [marked] as paid, consumers are extremely smart and [will] get upset about that. It's like the advertiser is trying to trick them. That is not the right way to do native advertising. Consumers are smart, and we [advertisers] need to be transparent about whether it is an editorial piece or whether it is paid messaging."

She's debating in her own mind whether or not transparency demands that advertisers include the brand in the headline or whether you make the headline about the content. She points out that there can be a negative reaction if you don't include the brand, because viewers feel duped, but she says even that depends on how explicitly the brand is brought into the article. She gave the example of an article about why you want to get the next refrigerator that was sponsored by Samsung, and it was all about the new Samsung fridge and none of its competitors, you'd probably want to be a little bit more explicit and put Samsung in the headline. On the other hand, if the article were about the features of the new Samsung fridge and all fridge options out there, you'd probably want to leave Samsung out of the headline.

RECOMMENDED GUIDELINES

Having now explored both publishers' and advertisers' takes on transparency and native advertising, let's take a look at some of the guidelines that are currently recommended.

Back in 2013, the Interactive Advertising Bureau (IAB) published a "Native Advertising Playbook," which I mentioned briefly in Chapter 1, in the discussion of "What Is Native Advertising?" This playbook included the following general recommendations for how native ads should be disclosed:

> For paid native ad units, clarity and prominence of the disclosure is paramount. The disclosure must:
> - Use language that conveys that the advertising has been paid for, thus making it an advertising unit, even if that unit does not contain traditional promotional advertising messages.
> - Be large and visible enough for a consumer to notice it in the context of a given page and/or relative to the device that the ad is being viewed on.

Simply put: Regardless of context, a reasonable consumer should be able to distinguish between what is paid advertising vs. what is publisher editorial content.[4]

The playbook also offers specific disclosures for five of the six types of native ads:

1. *In-feed ads* (which typically appear on BuzzFeed, Forbes Brand*Voice*, YouTube, Facebook, Twitter, Yahoo, Sharethrough, and LinkedIn) should have disclosures such as those listed at the beginning of this chapter.

2. *Search ads* (e.g., on Google, Yahoo, Bing) should use disclosures that state "ads related to _____ [whatever is being searched]."

3. *Recommendation widgets* typically use disclosures such as these:
   - "You might also like"
   - "You may have missed"
   - "Elsewhere from around the web"
   - "Recommended for you"

   For example: "Recommended by Outbrain" or "Sponsored content by Taboola."

4. *Promoted listings* (which typically appear on Google Promoted Listing Ads, Foursquare, and Amazon) should have disclosures like these:
   - "Ads" (with icon)
   - "Yelp Ad"
   - "Sponsored Products" (e.g., on Amazon)

- "Product Ads from External Websites"
- "Sponsored Content"

5. *In-Ad* (IAB Standard) content must have clearly defined borders and not be confused with normal web page content.

6. *Custom/Can't be contained* (everything else) disclosure for specifically custom type native advertising is not offered in the IAB Native Advertising Playbook and is instead covered by the IAB's overall guidance.

In June 2015, the Federal Trade Commission declared that publishers that are taking the role of an ad agency by creating content for marketers need to make sure they're not creating misleading native advertising: if that happens, the FTC will hold those publishers responsible. Mary Engle, the FTC's associate director of advertising practices, expressed the agency's concerns at an advertising industry conference: "For us, the concern is whether consumers recognize what they're seeing is advertising or not."[5] She then cited examples of native advertising on Buzz-Feed, Wired, and Gawker. And she clarified that the FTC is not censoring the *content* of native advertising, but is concerned with how clearly it is displayed and labeled on a site—for example, if an advertorial is labeled but in such a tiny font that it's easily overlooked by the average consumer.[6]

In December 2015, the FTC issued a 16-page "Enforcement Policy Statement on Deceptively Formatted Advertisements," which outlined the FTC's guidelines for ensuring that advertising (native or otherwise) is *not* deceptive. The introduction to the document sums up the FTC's position:

In determining whether an advertisement, including its format, misleads consumers, the Commission considers the overall "net impression" it conveys. Any qualifying information necessary to prevent deception must be disclosed prominently and unambiguously to overcome any misleading impression created.

The Commission has long held the view that advertising and promotional messages that are not identifiable as advertising to consumers are deceptive if they mislead consumers into believing they are independent, impartial, or not from the sponsoring advertiser itself. Knowing the source of an advertisement or promotional message typically affects the weight or credibility consumers give it. Such knowledge also may influence whether and to what extent consumers choose to interact with content containing a promotional message.[7]

The FTC policy statement went on to describe examples of advertising messages that it decided were deceptive over the past few decades, including:

- Advertorials in print publications that looked like news stories or feature articles
- Direct-mail ads that were disguised as book reviews
- Infomercials that seemed to be regular TV shows
- In-person sales pitches from people who didn't identify themselves as salespeople

The FTC provided further guidelines for how marketers and publishers should handle native advertising—essentially, by following these three points:

1. Transparency is the keyword.
2. Some native ads may be obvious ads; others may require a disclosure.
3. If a disclosure is necessary, it must be clear and prominent.[8]

These additional guidelines include 17 examples of advertising messages that do and do not require disclosures that they are, in fact, ads. If disclosures are required, they should be:

- in clear and unambiguous language;
- as close as possible to the native ads to which they relate;
- in a font and color that's easy to read;
- in a shade that stands out against the background;
- for video ads, on the screen long enough to be noticed, read, and understood; and
- for audio disclosures, read at a cadence that's easy for consumers to follow and in words consumers will understand[9]

In response to these guidelines, a few days following the FTC's publication of those guidelines, the IAB—the industry's trade association—weighed in with its view of those guidelines. IAB vice-president of public policy Brad Weltman said, "We very much appreciate the hard work the Commission has done to understand the issue of native advertising, and applaud the Commission for putting native advertising guidance into the marketplace. . . ." However, "the section on 'clarity of meaning' in native advertising disclosures is overly prescriptive."[10]

The IAB's Native Advertising Playbook recommends:

When evaluating native advertising options, marketers should ask six core questions to ensure that a unit will meet the brand's objectives:

1. **Form**—How does the ad fit with the overall page design? Is it in the viewer's activity stream or not in-stream?

2. **Function**—Does the ad function like the other elements on the page on which it is placed? Does it deliver the same type of content experience, e.g., a video on a video page or story among stories, or is it different?

3. **Integration**—How well do the ad unit's behaviors match those of the surrounding content? Are they the same, e.g., linking to an on-site story page, or are new ones introduced?

4. **Buying & targeting**—Is the ad placement guaranteed on a specific page, section, or site, or will it be delivered across a network of sites? What type of targeting is available?

5. **Measurement**—What metrics are typically used to judge success? Are marketers more likely to use top-of-the-funnel brand engagement metrics (e.g., views, likes, shares, time spent) or bottom funnel ones (e.g., sale, download, data capture, register, etc.?)

6. **Disclosure**—Is the disclosure clear and prominent?

CONSIDERATIONS FOR PUBLISHERS

Journalist Bill Densmore agrees with the FTC enforcement policy guidelines; in particular, that transparency is the key word. He doesn't believe that there is any First Amendment argument that says that we always have to know exactly who wrote something and what their economic interest in writing it is. Rather, he thinks the issue of transparency is not a legal issue as much as it is a business issue for publishers, who must consider to "what extent is your brand as a publisher and your ability to make money as a publisher going to be injured by the way in which you manage native advertising, by the way in which you lend the credibility of your brand to that of somebody doing a commercial speech?"

In Densmore's view, publishers need to consider what they have to do to protect and not dilute their brand at the same time that they're assisting advertisers speak to the public. His conclusion: "It's really important that there be a clear distinction between the commercial speech and the speech that's coming from the publishers themselves or some putatively public interest."

Satish Polisetti of AdsNative points out that the FTC rule on the disclosures came as no surprise to anyone in the industry. Almost a year after the rule was promulgated, he thought, "the publishers [were] doing a tremendously good job," and that they were ensuring that disclosure was, in fact, happening. "I don't see any publisher trying to hide their [native advertising.]" In his view, quality publishers are no longer trying to drive just any traffic; now they are looking for what he called authentic audiences, and "are doing the right things to ensure that the [audience's] engagement with these [online] experiences is authentic. . . . We've reached a stage in technology where everything can be tracked; everything can be measured, so nobody's trying to fool anybody [by using] very small disclosures [just to] get some clicks. . . . Everybody knows their strengths and weaknesses, and quality publishers are taking the right measures to [make] the disclosure [transparent]."

Polisetti went on to say that the same thing was true of advertisers. As he colorfully described it, "no brand is . . . saying, 'Do whatever it takes in order to give me 10 million clicks or 20 million video views.'"

Jeff Ratner of Zenith feels that despite the new FTC guidelines, the industry is still walking a fine line, and he is somewhat ambivalent about what the outcome may be. As he sees it, "the space is getting a bit blurred what [with] native ad units, those click-based boxes at the bottom of websites, and [the ways] different publishers try to monetize opportunities through platforms like Taboola. [They] are taking [what was] a pure idea around native, and turning it into clickbait, which is a challenge. I've wasted many hours clicking on those ads at the bottom of the pages, not realizing that they're ads." Although there are these new guidelines about differentiating an ad from content, Ratner thinks these may not do the trick, and we're probably going to see more of them.

From the standpoint of the consumer, Ratner believes the guidelines are beneficial, but he fears the industry might push going native too far and do it without giving the consumer some sort of heads-up that what they are viewing is a paid-for ad, in which, "we run the risk of both government and consumer backlash against it. That said, with ad blocking and ad skipping, we're almost giving the consumer a bit too much control in terms of their ability to consume content without paying the toll for that content, which is the interruption of an ad. There's going to be back and forth as it relates to advertising in general and native as to what's a reasonable expectation of a consumer's time for the value of the content that they're consuming."

Unlike Ratner, Lewis DVorkin of Forbes appears unconcerned about the FTC guidelines, although as pointed out earlier in the chapter, Forbes maintains a wall between advertising and journalism. "I don't think about them. Ever. I think the ship sailed, lost in space, moving forward. Things are changing so fast, and no regulatory agency seems capable of understanding the world of digital operations or publishing today. Maybe our sales guys [think about the guidelines], but I don't. . . . We have our own agenda. We believe we're clear and transparent." As DVorkin looks at it, it's perfectly clear whose content an article is because the name is included on the page.

From where DVorkin stands, "The native ad challenges for some companies are with the regulatory—banks are regulated. We have financial services companies who are BrandVoice partners, but there are definitely regulations that they have to deal with, which are not immaterial. Pharmaceutical companies have the same challenge."

Native advertising disclosure is important but complicated because there are a variety of native advertising categories. There are many companies involved, including: advertisers, their agencies, advertising technology companies, and publishers. There are several organizations developing standards and guidelines, including the FTC and the IAB.

CHALLENGES FOR HIGHLY
REGULATED INDUSTRIES

One industry that's having a difficult time doing native advertising is pharmaceuticals—even though many drug companies are chomping at the bit to do so—but they can't because of the disclosure requirements. In addition to FTC rules, pharmaceutical companies must also comply with FDA regulations.

Pharmaceutical companies are realizing (as all other companies are) that the "more overt forms of advertising are generally considered less engaging and effective"[11] than they once were (that is, if they ever were). Therefore, these companies are trying to become more customer-centric, and they're asking their advertising agencies to bring consumers into their branded content from whatever activity they would typically be doing online.

Jeff Sternstein, executive vice-president and director of client services for ad agency Havas-Lynx U.S., works with the pharmaceutical industry. He explained that pharmaceutical advertising has been in transition from being highly regulated in terms of what it could and could not say, as well as what it had to say in its advertising to being challenged to keep up with the more abbreviated forms of communications that exist in the digital age, like native advertising. Sternstein explains that in the past, if a pharmaceutical company wanted "to promote a new product in, let's say, a print ad, [they had to include] an enormous amount of what we call *fair balance* and *prescribing information*. Fair balance would be all the little disclaimers on the bottom of the page associated with the claims you're making in the ad [as well as] the prescribing information"; one to two to four full pages of fine print similar to what you'd find in a pharmaceutical package insert.

Over the past decade, Sternstein says, the FDA has attempted to allow the fair balance or "Important Safety Information" content to be shorter to focus on just a few of the major effects that might be of concern to people. The goal is to make the safety information more consumable, to have it stand out. According to Sternstein, that change has transformed the way pharmaceutical marketing is done, and, he says, the advent of the Internet and the spread of Google searches and the way people are searching for healthcare information has had an impact on the digital marketing landscape.

"We have to figure out how to do it," explains Sternstein. "Pharmaceutical advertising usually follows mass market advertising. [In this case,] we need to trailblaze. . . . Right now, I don't think native advertising [can] easily include some of the health and safety information that's required when you're making claims about a pharmaceutical product. . . . For pharmaceuticals, the challenge with native advertising is the encumbrance of having to have fair balance and prescribing information. . . .

"I could see a scenario where I could do native advertising for what would be an unbranded effort. When something is branded, you have to have with it all of the fair balance and prescribing information. . . . One technique could be starting with unbranded content. Let's say, 'The importance of vaccinating your preteen against HPV before they're sexually active,' that's the whole Gardasil campaign. Nowhere would Gardasil be mentioned. So the headline is, 'Attention, parents, things you should do to help protect your child in early adolescence.' You can go through a range of different things, including making sure they have the proper inoculations to keep them safe at this stage. When they were babies, you gave them rubella vaccines, and now that they're preteens, you should consider things like protecting against viruses that they can come across in their adolescence. Innocuous things. . . . And then you can click them to, 'To learn more, go to [this website].'

"So you go from the native advertising article to learn more at a website, and that website is all about protecting your teen and the different kinds of things that could help protect your teen, and it's brought to you by Gardasil." This offers the reader interesting content about the vaccine. It is important for the reader to know who authored and reviewed the content, including any influence on the content creation by the sponsor. Then, says Sternstein, "To learn more about products that can help you, click, and then you click into a branded environment. That's a hypothetical example. There has to be a certain number of clicks, a certain distance between the unbranded content that a person would find useful and the branded content that the clients are hoping people will engage with."

"Another little nuance is that you can't be the only product on the market for [that condition] and run an unbranded campaign, because if you're the only product on the market, it's implicitly a branded ad . . . and you need [to include] all the fair balance [information] associated with it."

Liquor is another highly regulated industry, which complicates how alcohol manufacturers go about native advertising. Jason Loehr is vice president, director of global media and insights for Brown-Forman, the $4.1 billion wine and spirits company with brands including Jack Daniel's whiskey, Finlandia vodka, and Korbel champagne (to name only a few). Loehr explained that the industry is guided by DISCUS (the Distilled Spirits Council of the United States), the trade association that governs all of the industry's advertising and marketing. (There are similar organizations in other countries.) One requirement is that the traffic to a site is of legal drinking age or above at a 71.6 percent perspective, which means that more than 71.6 percent of the people visiting the site are of legal drinking age. Brown-Forman uses partners like comScore to help validate those scores.

That leaves a little more than 28 percent of the site's visitors under age, but, according to Loehr, "those are the rules today. We're working with DISCUS on ways to . . . take a better approach . . . and [we believe] there's a very positive future, because . . . of . . . what we see [happening] and what we've done. . . . Jack Daniels Tennessee Honey was the first [alcoholic beverage] brand [to have a] promoted tweet. . . . At the time [2012], Twitter didn't have a way to [identify the age of someone on] their platform, so we created our own [way to get that information]. . . . If you followed Jack Daniels Tennessee Honey, you got a link and a direct message to go and validate your age, [if you didn't] you were actually unfollowed within 24 hours."

Since that first tweet social online media has expanded exponentially. Loehr believes that the time will come when third parties will be able to compile the data that's out there or where a consumer will create a profile containing their date of birth, so that brands like Jack Daniels will be able to ensure that the platforms they choose to advertise on in the future will have a percentage of viewers at or above the legal drinking age in the high nineties.

"We know that's an important thing, and our teams are working with DISCUS and our competitors and everyone that sits on that DISCUS Board to make that better, because we know, in the long run, we [will] have better tools."

For the present, Loehr continues, "The most important thing for us, at the end of the day, is to ensure that whatever the platform is, we are engaging in a conversation with someone who's of legal drinking age . . . that's the starting gate." Today, that means comScore and a couple of other sources that provide information about the demographics of each site's audience, in order to ascertain that there are no problems in terms of the age of the audience.

Once Jack Daniels knows the audience on a given platform is of the right age, they then must consider how the content and how those associated with it are perceived, and that the disclaimers are clear and transparent, because, Loehr says "on Twitter or Facebook, that sometimes can get lost, [which is not the case] if you're actually on the platform itself. [We] try to make sure that we are above board every step of the way and we try to ensure that what the [audience] sees is transparent, whether it's an ad or not."

Even though the platform has created the content for an ad and it's done natively in terms of its overall format and function inside the platform they've chosen, Loehr says they still have to ensure each of the things he mentioned is taken care of. For example, Loehr points to a native ad for Southern Comfort (a brand that Brown-Forman formerly owned) entitled, "14 Ways to Make an Awkward Date More Comfortable." At the bottom, the ad says,

"Please drink responsibly." "That's the most important thing for us; that last bit that talks about responsibility. 'Live comfortably, drink responsibly,' is one of the big tags for Southern Comfort, so ensuring that [was included was essential], because . . . it's recognized as an ad. So we have to make sure it . . . includes everything." He concludes by saying, "We definitely try not to dupe the consumer and follow all of the different regulations that have been enacted since the industry started doing [native] advertising, but I can see how some people [might] think [otherwise]."

The food industry is another highly regulated industry. Not only is it regulated by the FTC rules related to native advertising, it is also subject to the FDA regulations as well as by industry-imposed standards. Heather Dumford says ConAgra belongs to a group that says members will not advertise explicitly to children unless their products meet certain health requirements, "which we follow to a *T*. So it's less about general advertising; it's more about kids under six, [and the rules are] a little bit easier to follow than [those] the alcohol [industry has to follow]."

NEW QUESTIONS TO COME

These are provocative issues, and with the proliferation of native advertising, they will probably not be resolved to anyone's satisfaction in the short term. More likely, each new guideline and each new technology will raise new questions. Advertising technology has created an opaque environment where consumers are challenging publishers with ad blocking and advertisers are challenging their agencies to become more transparent about the media fulfillment process. This represents a breakdown of trust. Similarly, in the future, major trust problems will develop if native advertising transparency standards are not evolved and adopted by industry practitioners.

CHAPTER 5

HOW JOURNALISTS

ARE ADAPTING

While marketers, advertisers, brand managers, and publishers are cheering the advent and increase of native advertising, many journalists are not so happy. This chapter takes a look at both the "old guard" of traditional writers (who began their careers by writing for paper-based publications) and the "young Turks" (who are just graduating from journalism schools and starting their careers), to see how they feel about how native advertising is changing the way publications handle content. Many are finding they need to either adapt or adopt new ways of working.

The primary question asked of journalists was, "Is native advertising the 'new normal'?" I wanted to know their opinions, especially since native advertising seems to appeal most to millennials—people born between the late 1980s and early 2000s, who grew up with digital communication—in contrast to older writers who literally started their careers on typewriters.[1] And I received a range of answers—from nostalgia for the way things used to be to acceptance that there's a whole new way to communicate both informational and entertainment content, regardless of who writes or sponsors it: in other words, as long as it informs or entertains, it's OK.

Nevertheless, one ex-journalist (whom I won't name here) said that when he first saw native advertising making inroads into traditional publishing:

> I was depressed. I thought we had one more nail in the coffin of the journalism business, and there have been many nails, at this point. Certainly I think that journalism, when practiced the right way, is a valuable tool and a fantastic way to

get a sense of what's really going on in the world. [But] when you devolve to a *Huffington Post* style where it's all basically eye candy, with some good stuff thrown in, it's not the same thing. So I think it's too bad that companies are forced to actually do this.

In fact, many traditional journalists felt not only anguish about native advertising but antipathy toward digital publishing in general, as this same ex-journalist described:

When we started [the online version of our print publication], there was a huge amount of pushback from the editorial side at [the print] magazine. They thought we were publishing stuff that wasn't very serious, and, in many ways, they were right, but the fact of the matter is that we had a different business model. We did not have the kind of resources [that the print version had]. We had a huge editorial hole that we had to fill on a daily basis, not just on a weekly basis, so we did whatever we could to find readers or create content that readers would actually want to read. The problem is that most people want to read light stuff. For the most part, you will not find people committing themselves to read a 4,000-word piece on politics or Chinese business. . . . People are more apt to find out what Kim Kardashian is doing, and that's too bad, but unfortunately that's how the game changed.

Of course, one of the benefits of online publications is that publishers can track who is reading what—for example, more people are more likely to read about celebrities in Hollywood or music than, say, what's happening on the Forex market, or in commodities investing. As a subject becomes more specialized, it naturally will appeal to a narrower audience than the general reading public.

It's important to keep in mind, though, that there has always been a rivalry between editors and auditors, if you will—the money side of the business. This situation hasn't arisen with the advent of digital publishing, or even with the increase in native advertising; few publications can afford to be nonprofits. As one interviewee summed up (anonymously):

The editorial side used to be able to afford to be as high-minded as it was because times were relatively good. They didn't have to worry, *Will there be enough advertising? Will we have enough money?* When the ads were coming in, in pre-Internet days, when there weren't a lot of other ways for advertisers to reach high-net worth clients, magazines like *BusinessWeek* and *Forbes* were rolling in it. So the editorial side could even afford to . . . piss off advertisers if there was an article that was critical of Exxon [for example], and if Exxon got mad and pulled its ads, they could say, 'Too bad, because we've got plenty of other people who are going to come around and fill those ad pages. We don't need you. You need us.' Then that all changed. . . . If I were on the business side of a magazine or a website or any kind of media outlet, at this point, I would be very mindful of about how incredibly difficult it is to make any money at all, and if native advertising was something I had to use, I would use it.

Still, the changes in the journalism world that were brought about first by digital publishing and then by native advertising and branded content were bemoaned by several journalists interviewed for this book. One said when he gets together with former coworkers and talks about the industry, "We laugh in a sad way about how it's changed. We shake our heads and stare grimly into our beers . . . [as] someone who grew up in the traditional church-and-state divide, I'm more inclined to be critical of what has happened than not."

However, he also said he understands the financial necessities of publishing today. "Having been in the business, and having friends on both sides of the wall, . . . I know how hard the marketers [and] sales guys work. Their ass is on the line all the time, and it's gotten worse, so they are doing everything that they can to squeeze every last penny. So if native advertising is a way to go, [it's OK] as long as there is a hat tip that shows, from a graphic design point of view, that this is not the same thing [as the publication's regular content]. It's not the worst thing in the world. The worst thing in the world is when people lose their jobs, when magazines go dark. So if you have to come up with what might be a sleazy or questionable way to get around [that], to make sure that people can afford to pay their rent, then that's not such a bad thing."

Another long-time journalist had this to say:

At first, we were very apprehensive about what would happen with this thing—giving [brands] equal footing on the page to write. But what we discovered, and what a lot of marketers discovered, was *it's very hard to write things that people want to read,* even if you were given access to write whatever you want. . . . Say you're a networking company, and you want to [write] about the future of the Internet, it's one thing to get the opportunity to do that; it's another thing to actually write anything that anybody wants to read. That's the trick.

Another journalist with a long and successful career at a variety of print and digital publications had a really interesting response. Lewis DVorkin was lambasted in some early articles about native advertising: one even went so far as to say he was "destroying journalism." When asked what his reaction to this was, he politely and quietly responded, "I didn't care."

Another former journalist had this to say:

I think people are appalled by what they're seeing, and I guess I'm appalled at what publishers feel they have to do to stay viable. But on the other hand, the bottom line is the bottom line, and the first requirement is to stay in business, and sometimes you have to do things to stay in business in the short term that may have unintended consequences in the long term. I think it's those unintended consequences in the long term that we have to all be thinking about and figuring out if we can measure somehow. Because if the end-game of the *New York Times* running sponsored advertising is that the *New York Times* loses its brand value, then what's the point of having that short-term revenue? [On the other hand] . . . if you can preserve the values, principles, and purposes of the *New York Times* . . . and help commercial brands produce and present native advertising, then that's great. [But you need to preserve the publication's] reputation for integrity and its intention not to be influenced in any clandestine way by commercial forces.

NEW JOURNALISTS' VIEWS

Many of the very young journalists interviewed for this book were only familiar with the term *native advertising* from their classes. However, when they read native advertisements, they knew they were ads, not regular editorial content; they were simply unfamiliar with the term. One budding journalist said she simply thought she was reading "a well-written advertisement." But now that she knows more about native, she said, "I'm definitely more aware of it—and even more critical of how it's done."

In one class, the discussion focused on how native advertising was being done and whether or not it was ethical. As one student said, "It's almost like tricking the reader if you don't actually show that it is an advertisement."

Another recent grad said she didn't feel tricked when she first saw native ads in print magazines, especially in fashion and beauty magazines. She felt many were so "seamlessly integrated into the rest of the magazine's content" in the way they were laid out and how they used accompanying pictures. As a result, she didn't feel she was "being interrupted" by ads. Instead, it was more of a "natural progression." As she phrased it, she wasn't thinking, "I'm being advertised to"; instead, she simply thought, "I'm just reading something new." Again, she felt native ads were simply a more seamless way for a company to advertise their products.

LEARNING ABOUT NATIVE
ADVERTISING

Although native advertising seems to be covered in undergraduate classes on marketing and advertising, it may not be explicitly covered in graduate journalism programs. For example, one young professional pursuing a master's in journalism said his curriculum didn't address native advertising—but that's because his MA program focuses on subject matter expertise rather than skills. He said "[Native advertising] has quickly become something that is just part of how publishers do business in the digital age. There's not a lot of doom and gloom and fretting about it. It's not going to be our job [referring to journalists in the newsroom]. It's the publishers' job, so that's for them to worry about."

However, although the topic wasn't being covered in his curriculum, he is "very familiar" with the term and the practice of native advertising. He recalled the early days of native ads, when there were advertorials in print publications—for example, exhorting readers on the benefits of buying gold—and he was aware of the "debacle" of the *Atlantic* magazine and what was revealed to be a native ad on Scientology (which I discussed in Chapter 3).

This journalist even reported on trends in native: he said he's "intrigued" by it because it's "something new, something the industry is trying to figure out . . . that potentially holds a lot of promise for making digital journalism viable as a business." From his own research on native advertising, he found that demand is really rising, which he attributed at least partially to how the Internet as a whole is changing. He described how five or 10 years ago, it was fairly easy for a company to create a company blog, hire a blogger to write and publish a few stories on that blog, and actually get a lot of traffic through search optimization and social media.

Unfortunately, that's not really doable anymore: "The web is getting very crowded," and there's so much content that it's increasingly difficult for a company or a brand to publish its own blog and get any kind of traction or build an audience, the way commercial publishers do. Because major newspapers and magazines (such as the *New York Times* or *Forbes*) still have large built-in audiences, it may make more sense for a brand to pay those publications, if they want to reach those readers, rather than try and build that readership from scratch on their own websites or blogs.

Another young journalist said native advertising doesn't bother her, as long as it's not blatant promotion that's trying to pass for objective third-party editorial content. She cited two contrasting examples. I mentioned her first example in Chapter 4: it was a listicle that purported to provide how-to information, but every suggestion it offered concluded with the suggestion that readers buy a product at a well-known national retailer. Once she realized that, she stopped reading, since she felt the article was just a pitch for that retailer. Moreover, she said that happens to her at least once a day. Of the dozens of articles she reads every day, from a myriad of websites, she'll typically abandon at least one every day because it's so obviously promotional rather than informational and unbiased.

However, she also cited an opposing example, an article on how to become better organized. In this case, she said it wasn't until the end of the article that she even realized that it was a sponsored post, from 3M, promoting its Post-it products. Although the article was labeled at the top "Sponsored Post" (or something to that effect), she overlooked that heading. And the article was so well-written and balanced that it didn't seem like a plug for just one particular product. In fact, there were many other products mentioned in the article, as well, which made it informative and useful to her.

This is the same type of balance that Kate Lewis cited (also in Chapter 4), when she described the branded content that Maybelline had done in conjunction with Hearst Magazines Digital Media. The key to the success of this type of content is that it is not promoting only one particular brand but features multiple brands, so that readers can decide for themselves which products they're interested in. In this way, the native ads are well received by the writers, the publishers, the brands sponsoring them, and ultimately the readers.

ARE JOURNALISTS WILLING TO *CREATE* NATIVE ADVERTISING?

Although all these young people had no problem *reading* native advertising, they were divided in their views about whether or not they would be willing to get a job *creating* it.

One journalist said he didn't want to write native ads because that didn't fit into his ambition of developing a career in journalism. He did concede that writing native ads may require the same skill set as traditional journalism—writers need to understand their audience and have strong storytelling abilities. He also recognized that many very well-regarded traditional publications now have entire departments devoted to native advertising—including the *New York Times* (T Brand Studio) and the *Washington Post* (WP Brand Studio), to name only two of the largest U.S. newspapers. Nevertheless, when asked if he would take a job writing native ads, he replied bluntly, "No. It's not something that I would do."

However, he also conceded that people who are just starting out in their careers—including himself—could be swayed or persuaded to write advertisements. As he put it, "Let's be honest, everybody will take a job for a certain price." Referring to a small publication where he had worked, he added, "If they had offered me a truckload of money, I can't say I would never accept it."

He also confirmed much of what was discussed in Chapter 4 (and elsewhere in this book): that the most critical component of native advertising is the *disclosure* that it is indeed advertising. He said publications simply need to be "honest and transparent" about what is editorial content that is written by a publication's staff of writers and editors and what is paid-for content that is created by a brand or a company as advertising.

Finally, he admitted that even though he wouldn't want to write native ads, he's glad native advertising exists, because it's a revenue model that will allow publications to pay journalists in the future. In this view, he was in agreement with another 'old-guard' journalist I mentioned earlier, who said that native advertising "isn't the worst thing in the world." Again, the worst thing is for publications to "go dark" and fail—resulting, of course, in everyone who worked for those publications losing their jobs—all because the publications didn't have enough money (i.e., enough advertising revenue) coming in to keep them afloat.

THE POSITIVE SIDE OF WRITING
NATIVE ADVERTISING

As mentioned, not everyone interviewed felt this way, not even among the journalists just beginning their careers. One said she would consider writing native advertising "depend[ing] on how much control I had over it. If I could write something that was good quality and didn't push the product or service, . . . I might be fine with that." She added, that she would "definitely" want the article to be labeled as native advertising or sponsored content.

Another person just embarking on her journalism career said she "definitely would consider" writing native ads. She took a lot of marketing classes, and although "a lot of people sometimes say that marketing and advertising is the work of the devil, I find it super interesting, and I really enjoy studying consumer behavior." As a result, writing native ads would be a nice blend of marketing and editorial for her.

She said native ads "never bothered me" when she encountered them, and she didn't feel she was "being bombarded with ads all the time." Although "people think my generation [is] not so interested in what marketers have to say . . . [I'm intrigued by] the new techniques that marketers are starting to develop in order to target my generation [and to] make [native advertising] seamless." She mentioned a few websites that integrate native ads into their content really well, most notably BuzzFeed, and she said on those sites, native ads have "been effective in enticing me as a consumer."

In fact, she even purchased some of the products she read about in native ads, so those ads were obviously effective. And it's likely that's another reason she would consider writing ads instead of traditional journalism.

Digital media has had a major impact on journalism. Content companies like Hearst and Forbes and distribution "platform" companies like Google, Facebook, and Snapchat need to work together to ensure that objective journalism can be financed by advertising including native advertising.

CHAPTER 6

A LOOK AT BRANDS THAT

HAVE GONE NATIVE

This chapter provides information from marketers who are doing native advertising on a wide variety of sites. Consider this "from the horse's mouth," so to speak: it includes insights from companies that sell everything from technology to food to cars to "spirits" (otherwise known, for those of us not working in this industry, as alcoholic beverages). I'll provide information on how much of the total marketing budget is devoted to native advertising; how companies come up with ideas and the execution of the native ads; and examples from different companies in different industries.

My job is in digital advertising for Hearst, and I am also a consumer of media. Throughout each day, I read content from a variety of publications on my different mobile devices.

Before I ever thought about writing this book, I remember asking people which native ads they were familiar with. I wanted to gauge how familiar people were with this phenomenon. Not surprisingly, I discovered that, outside of the advertising world, few people even knew what a native ad was. That said, however, many people were familiar with the listicles that appear on their social media feeds. So I started digging into what other people were looking at, and I found a surprising but nonetheless interesting treasure trove of content.

First, of course, there were pet listicles. For example, "11 Things Your Cat Is Desperately Trying to Tell You"—such as "3 a.m. is actually wake-up time, and you've been doing it wrong forever." Accompanied by cute cat cartoons and additional clever cat captions, this quick read is brought to you by PetSafe, a company that makes electronic pet equipment (such as automatic pet feeders and self-cleaning litter boxes). The graph at the end of the listicle indicates that 84 percent of people who read this gave it a heart emoji, though it doesn't indicate how many people read or looked at it. Moreover, people added their own comments about which items apply to their own cats; one reader even wrote in imploring, "Do one for dogs!"

Next, I checked out "11 Horrifying Bathroom Facts Told by Something Cute," which was created by Scrubbing Bubbles. This listicle informed me that "a bathroom hand dryer is basically a germ tornado," which I found disappointing, since the whole idea behind hand dryers in public bathrooms is to make them cleaner (less trash), though it seems this is at the expense of *our* cleanliness. I'm not sure what I'm going to do with that information, but I appreciate knowing it.

Finally on BuzzFeed, I read "11 Cocktails that Will Turn up Your Summer Party," courtesy of Svedka Vodka. I'm happy to know how to persuade my guests to eat such healthy fruits as strawberries, pineapples, and mangos at my next barbecue—by mixing them into my vodka drinks, of course.

I recognized that these listicles are all pretty light content, and I know there must be more serious informative content being provided by companies making more sophisticated products than what's being promoted here. So I turned to the experts: people who work in marketing and advertising at a variety of different companies in a broad spectrum of industries. I wanted to know—as I'm sure you do, too—whether there are any particular industries that more naturally gravitate to native advertising, and I wanted to know how different companies approach this part of their marketing and advertising budget.

Most of the people interviewed for this book wouldn't reveal how much of that budget was devoted to native advertising. Many said (very quickly though still politely) that their companies simply don't/won't disclose that information. When pressed, however, they indicated that it's still a "very small" part of the total budget. One marketing person did come clean, which I appreciated, and admitted it's only about three to five percent. For some reason—I don't know why, perhaps just gut instinct—I believe that figure is probably true for most companies, at least as of right now. And when I searched online for confirmation, that's what I found: 68 percent of 127 marketers surveyed by the Association of National Advertisers (ANA) said that native advertising represents only five percent or less of their budgets.[1]

The following information is relevant because it illustrates an increase in the amount of native advertising and branded content consumers will be exposed to going forward, along with concerns about transparency. Here are a few more interesting statistics from this same survey that indicate:

- 63 percent of marketers planned to increase their budgets earmarked for native advertising in 2015 (the survey was conducted in the fourth quarter of 2014).
- 55 percent of respondents had increased their budgets in 2014.
- Spending on native ads was predicted to reach $4.3 billion in 2015 (presumably, this is in the United States, although the article didn't specify), according to eMarketer, which represented a 34 percent increase over the previous year.

- Two-thirds of respondents to this survey felt that native advertising needs clear disclosure.
- Three-fourths of respondents feel there is an ethical boundary for the advertising industry in relation to native advertising.

Since Chapter 4 discussed the ethics and disclosures issue in detail, let's skip these last two points and take a look at who's doing what. Even if it is only three to five percent of the budget, a $4.3 billion market in digital advertising that is growing is material.

Let's begin by looking at the market. Many people interviewed for this book mentioned that the primary target market for native advertising is millennials—the demographic born between the late 1980s and early 2000s. Since most of what this book focuses on is *digital* native advertising, that certainly makes sense. After all, anyone under age 35 at the time of this writing grew up in a digital world. Anyone older than that remembers what it was like to use a phone that is now referred to as a "landline" or a typewriter, which of course preceded computers in the office.

Jason Loehr at Brown-Forman said the brand his company probably did the most native advertising for was Southern Comfort (which Brown-Forman sold in January 2016 as part of its efforts to focus on its highest strategic priorities). It developed a series of short videos that appeared mostly on BuzzFeed, which reaches the audience that matches the Southern Comfort target demographic.

The campaign was called "Whatever's Comfortable," and the first videos featured a middle-aged, mustachioed man with a bit of a paunch hanging over his maroon Speedo bathing suit as he walks slowly and confidently down a beach. Eventually, he picks up an old-fashioned glass of Southern Comfort and continues his walk, accompanied by an old bluesy folk tune called "Hit or Miss," sung by Odetta Holmes (with the lyric, "Ain't nobody just like me; I gotta be me"). These ads first appeared around 2012, but the unidentified actor developed a following, so more videos were created.

Southern Comfort also developed a series of listicles that also tapped into the idea of comfort. For example, "14 Ways to Make an Awkward Date More Comfortable," which includes advice like "When they look *very* different from their profile picture," compliment your date, note how much he or she has matured since that picture was taken, and offer to take a *new* picture. All the "advice" is silly and is accompanied by cute and clever videos either of young people who appear to be out on a date or from old movies (for example, Buster Keaton cutting his spaghetti with scissors, from a 1918 movie, to illustrate how to handle a date with unusual eating habits).

Loehr described these native ads as successful in terms of sociability and shareability, as well as other measures his company looks at in terms of how people engage with and share the content. He did admit that "there were some folks who wondered, *Is this too much of a leap?* or *what's the risk involved here?* But as we got into it and saw the content and how it connected, it ended up being a pretty great case study internally of how we looked at native advertising."

Southern Comfort is not the only brand Brown-Forman has done native advertising for (as mentioned, the company sold that brand in early 2016). Brown-Forman also did native ads for Jack

Daniels whiskey and for Woodford Reserve, a small-batch bourbon. Brown-Forman works with Starcom Mediavest Group (part of the Publicis Group), which handles the company's media planning and buying in 18 markets globally (including the United States). The company focuses primarily on its top brands that do a lot of above-the-line advertising. Loehr also points out that the company is most interested in developing native ads that are "bespoke" and specific to its brands, so that the ads are not something where you could simply replace, for example, Jack Daniel's with some other whiskey made by some other company. Similarly, the Southern Comfort ads were created around the idea of "Whatever's Comfortable," which tied into the name and the feeling of that particular brand.

Loehr estimates that about 5 to 10 percent of Brown-Forman's advertising is native advertising: in "the new/now/next model, it's probably in that new/next category," although it also varies by brand and by market, especially in different countries. In some markets, a huge portion of the budget goes to digital advertising, whereas in others, TV is an option because the regulations change across markets in different countries. As he put it, "The digital piece is a great rifle that allows us to be very precise, [whereas] TV is a traditional platform that's more an elephant gun with a very large, wide blast." For example, the "Whatever's Comfortable" campaign for Southern Comfort ran on TV as well as on Facebook, Google, Twitter, and some of the larger platforms. In addition, there were native campaigns (like the one on BuzzFeed), which complemented the main campaign nicely but was also a bit different in terms of the audience, because BuzzFeed attracts a younger audience than other platforms.

BRANDTALE'S DATABASE OF
BRANDED CONTENT

As mentioned earlier in the book, Ben Darr and Jay Widlitz are cofounders of Brandtale, which Darr describes as "a database of every piece of branded content on social and web that is created between brands and content creators. If we were doing this for print magazines, our site would be a collection of every print insert that a brand did in a magazine." Before they founded their company, Darr and Widlitz worked for Thrillist Media Group (whose website identifies Thrillist as an online publication for guys, "the essential resource for how to spend your time and money," covering "all the stuff you love—food, drink, travel, cars, sex, dating, health and entertainment"). They developed Brandtale while still working at Thrillist to help the sales team with competitive insights as to who was doing what, where; "Then it snowballed," according to Widlitz, and they realized "there was such a strong need for the industry" that they started growing the publisher list and left to devote themselves to Brandtale full-time.

Brandtale now works with more than 400 publishers and the thousands of brands those publishers work with on branded content and native advertising. The end goal is, according to Widlitz, to "dissect insights and learnings from the macro data to give people more tools to do research, sales prospecting, and hopefully grow their businesses." Initially, the information was free, but in early 2016, the founders rebuilt their site and now make their information available only via a paid subscription, though there is still a free 10-day trial available, to entice new users to the value of the site.

Publishers are increasing their revenues by offering native advertising products to their client advertisers and agencies. Brandtale is a very effective tool for both sales prospecting and learnings about best practices. Users of Brandtale can search the site by the name of a publication, by type of publication (e.g., lifestyle, business, etc.), by brand name, by category (e.g., ads regarding sports or entertainment), and/or by industry (e.g., all alcohol brands or all auto brands, etc.). The company's goal is to offer the most flexibility to users so they can discover branded content and learn more about native advertising. Widlitz claims Brandtale is "the only company that actually captures the experience between the brand and the publisher."

The site's customers include publishers; brands; advertising agencies (particularly media agencies); and ad-tech companies that want to understand what smart brands and publishers are doing, who's spending money and when they're spending it, and what stories are they trying to tell. These companies often use the information to prospect for new customers of their own. In short, as Widlitz sums up, Brandtale's customers encompass "pretty much everybody who's in the space." That includes publishers that are naturally interested in what other publishers are doing, so they can track their competition. Brands are interested because more brands are taking their content in-house and producing it themselves, so they want to keep up with who's doing the best work. In the native ad space, distribution companies (e.g., Bidtellect, TripleLift) are interested because they serve in-feed ads and bring in outside demand to make publishers more money. Finally, companies that deal in branded content (such as NewsCred and Contently) are also interested. Publishers should evaluate the opportunities these companies might offer their businesses.

Widlitz commented that every industry has tried doing native advertising—and in every industry, some companies do more native advertising than others. According to Darr, the industries that have really taken hold and spent a lot of money on native advertising are finance, electronics and technology, alcohol brands, and auto brands. Widlitz added that the finance industry is typically doing content marketing to provide advice or insights to potential customers. The alcohol, auto, and technology industries tend to create brand-building interactive experiences. Widlitz mentioned Microsoft and Oracle as doing great work in native advertising because they are providing good information that helps people make smarter decisions about technology.

During 2016, Darr said Brandtale saw an increase in NGOs and other government- and policy-focused brands doing more native advertising, which may have been spurred by the U.S. presidential election. Travel brands are very cyclical, as are fashion brands and retailers, which tend to spend enormously on advertising during the fourth quarter of a year, which is their big season.

WHAT BRANDS ARE DOING
IT PARTICULARLY WELL?

Darr also cited a few finance companies that are doing great work in native advertising, most notably Goldman Sachs, State Farm, and J.P. Morgan Chase. These companies have been investing in branded content for more than two years, which enabled them to figure out early on what works and what doesn't, so they are now in their stride. In addition, Ford, Toyota, and Lexus are a few auto brands that Darr thinks are doing a great job with native advertising. Finally, he cited Netflix and Warner Brothers as two entertainment brands that have learned quickly which partners they want to invest their native advertising budgets with. He also pointed out that many of these companies' ad agencies are handling only the media buying, which is why publishers have stepped in to offer their creative services to develop the content and ads themselves.

SOME SECTORS TO WATCH

As mentioned earlier, Adam Kasper's Havas clients include Fidelity Investments, LVMH (Louis Vuitton Moët Hennessy, the world's leading luxury-goods conglomerate), Sears, Panasonic, Volvo, and many others. Kasper cited the fashion, beauty, and retail industries as doing more native advertising than, say, the finance industry. He believes the finance sector may not do as much native as other industries because of regulation issues, which are likely to slow down content development and approvals. In addition, he thinks more and more verticals are moving toward native and away from highly produced 30-second television commercials.

Like Darr and Widlitz, Kasper sees more native advertising being created by publishers (rather than traditional advertising agencies) because they "can get more done directly with a publisher these days than [they] ever could before in terms of creating content."

HEWLETT-PACKARD

Ed McLoughlin, Global Head of Media and Data Science for Hewlett-Packard, said HP's most successful work in native advertising has been done mostly by social influencers who develop content on HP's behalf. Most of these influencers are millennials who have millions of followers on Facebook, Vine, Instagram, Snapchat, or other sites. These influencers are totally transparent to their followers and fans that HP is providing them with products (computers, etc.) on which they can create content or is somehow otherwise sponsoring the content they create. For example, HP might approach an influencer and describe a new product and its features—for example, an HP notebook that rotates in 360 degrees. Then, the influencer creates some content around that idea, promotes the content to his or her follower base, with a tag line somewhere that reads something like "thanks to HP for allowing us to showcase these products."

In working this way, HP relinquishes some control to these influencers; however, on the upside, because the influencers are transparent about their relationship with HP, their content comes across as "natural" to their audiences. In other words, it doesn't come across as in-your-face advertising. Some of these influencers are minor celebrities, but most are simply people who are creating photography or videos that they post and which attract a following.

For example, HP worked with Sara Mearns, a young up-and-coming dancer who is a principal ballerina with the New York City Ballet. She's not yet a household name, but according to McLoughlin, she had about 30,000 followers on Instagram when HP approached her about doing something to promote the new HP x2, which is a detachable 10-inch PC that offers four modes of working: a notebook for work, a tablet to go, a stand to watch, and a tent to play. The result is a two-minute video (on YouTube as well as other sites) that shows Sara dancing in a practice studio to electronic music provided by DJ "LCAW" as they ping ideas back and forth to each other on the HP x2. Essentially, HP sponsors Sara to promote new HP products, to reach the millennial audience they're targeting for these products.

Another example of HP's influencers comes from Robby Ayala, a 24-year-old "Vine star" with 3.5 million followers who started creating Vines when he was in law school, simply to break up the boredom of study hall. His Vines began to attract more and more attention: 5,000 views, then 10,000 views, and then they really started growing. In his Vine for HP, we see him watching a young woman snap the screen off her HP Pavilion x360 convertible laptop, so he does the same with his laptop, which unfortunately is *not* convertible, as he discovers when he breaks it into two pieces. The caption reads, "So I found out today that not all laptops convert into a tablet" as he looks on with horror at what he has just done.

This Vine was part of HP's "Bend the Rules" campaign: HP commissioned 30 Vine posts, which resulted in 950,000 active engagements and 50 million organic views. Robby Ayala's Vine for the campaign received 232,400 likes, 115,100 reVines, 6,700 comments, and 12.3 million loops. HP also used 5 Vines to create a U.S. TV commercial that ran for five and a half weeks and was even shown in French movie theaters.[2]

McLoughlin said HP is always on the lookout for fresh voices—new influencers with large follower bases, since many of these content creators tend to peak and then wane. So the company needs to cast a wide net.

Because HP is trying to drive reach among its target audience by working with social influencers, the challenge is that although each may have 2 to 3 million followers, McLoughlin pointed out that still requires HP to cobble together 10 or 12 such influencers in order to get any scale. As a result, like other companies mentioned at the beginning of this chapter, HP's spend on native advertising is "relatively small" in relation to the company's total marketing and advertising budget. So although native drives HP's social strategy, the company still advertises via traditional media—in print, on TV, and in traditional digital media to drive most of its reach. McLoughlin estimated that native is probably much less than 10 percent, and perhaps only about five percent of the company's total budget.

In addition, people (and technologies) continue to find new ways to skip ads—whether through DVRs where users can skip TV commercials, or by watching TV on Netflix or Amazon, which have no commercials because users pay a subscription fee, or by using ad-blocking apps on their web browsers. So companies need to continue to find new ways to get their messages across to consumers, so that the message feels relevant but is not disruptive. As content that people read or watch becomes less and less supported by traditional advertising, there's going to be more and more native integration into content and programming. As McLoughlin sums up, native advertising is "just another tactic in our arsenal to reach consumers."

GE AND MARRIOTT

Alexa Christon described how GE has worked with many partners on native advertising programs. In each case, the company creates a new experience for the specific audience that each publishing partner is best suited to reach.

For example, in November 2015, the *New York Times* sent a Google Cardboard virtual reality (VR) headset with the week's "Sunday Magazine" from the *New York Times* to one million subscribers of the print edition of the *Times*. This campaign was done in conjunction with the *Times'* T Brand Studios: GE created original virtual reality content that ran alongside editorial content, which was then promoted with native content as well on nytimes .com. The VR headset would showcase a story from the *New York Times* about children uprooted by war, and a separate story from GE about technology inspired by nature.[3]

GE chose to partner with the *New York Times* to reach a mass audience and to introduce them to new technology that allows viewers to experience a story in a whole new way—the medium being the message.

Christon couldn't divulge GE's advertising and marketing budget devoted to native advertising, and she emphasized that GE doesn't think in those terms. She realizes that many companies are interested in or in the process of creating a content marketing team, but at GE, "everyone in marketing thinks about content," about how to create an experience that will resonate with people. There's no individual content marketing manager or content marketing team. Instead, developing brand content and native advertising is part of the job for everyone working in marketing at GE.

Christon noted a few other companies that she thinks are doing native advertising well. One is Marriott, which she feels has done some interesting work, especially around VR content. The other is Netflix, which "has had some interesting wins with the *New York Times.*" With Netflix, I presume she's referring to the native ad piece sponsored by *Orange Is the New Black*, which so many people interviewed for this book have cited.

Regarding Marriott, I investigated a little further once she cited the hotel chain, and I found that Marriott won a Webby Award (for excellence on the Internet) in 2015 for a native ad campaign that it produced on Reddit. Marriott asked Reddit users to write or film "sales pitches" that would describe what makes their neighborhoods special—either because they love their community or hate it—and then post them on Reddit. Marriott enticed Reddit users to do this by offering "a vacation of a lifetime" with $4,000 to spend on flights and a stay at a Marriott hotel and the opportunity to try out the company's 4-D virtual travel experience, where they can be "teleported" to the place of their dreams. The campaign was so successful that Marriott received almost 200,000 clicks on its contest page and Reddit's highest-ever user-generated content for sponsored posts.[4]

PHARMACEUTICALS

One industry that would like to do more native advertising but has faced some obstacles is pharmaceuticals. The challenge the big drug companies face when attempting native advertising is the regulations. Think of all the "fine print" information that pharmaceutical companies need to disclose when pitching a new product. For example, in a 60-second TV commercial for the drug Humira, to treat joint pain and psoriatic arthritis, almost *half* of the time describing the drug is used to provide disclosures like these: "Humira can lower your ability to fight infections, including tuberculosis. Serious, sometimes fatal infections and cancers, including lymphoma, have happened, as have blood, liver, and nervous systems problems, serious allergic reactions, and new or worsening heart failure. . . . Don't start Humira if you have an infection."[5] That type of extensive disclosure of possible side effects and risk factors is difficult to build into a native advertisement, according to Jeff Sternstein, who works on ad campaigns for many pharmaceutical companies. Although those companies can't do native ads for specific drugs, they can do—and have done—a considerable amount of unbranded advertising that worked well.

For example, Pfizer and Boehringer Ingelheim (a German-based pharmaceutical giant that makes, among many other drugs, Zantac for stomach-acid relief and Dulcolax for relief from constipation) had partnered to develop Spiriva, which is used to treat people with COPD (chronic obstructive pulmonary disease), which includes chronic bronchitis and emphysema and has become the fourth-largest killer in the world. The two pharmaceuticals companies wanted to increase awareness of COPD and the lack of control that people currently had over their condition, so they ran a campaign called "Drive for COPD." This campaign ran online and on TV; the ads focused on people taking a simple test, of 5 to 10 questions about their health, to find out if they have COPD. Because Spiriva is a leader in the treatment of COPD, the drug companies benefited because if someone found out he or she had COPD, there was a pretty good chance that person would be prescribed Spiriva instead of other products. There were also ways of linking from "Drive for COPD" through a path of clicks to learn more about Spiriva.

Therefore, in the pharmaceuticals industry (and probably many other industries), native advertising fits into the top of the marketing "funnel." In other words, it targets the broadest audience a marketer wants to engage with. Because the funnel narrows from top to bottom, native advertising in this COPD example will first reach people who are interested in understanding what's wrong with their breathing, then people who may have COPD, then people who are motivated to see a doctor, then people whose doctors test them and diagnose them with COPD, and finally people who are prescribed Spiriva. As a result, Sternstein thinks native advertising works very well in filling the top of the funnel, to reach people not necessarily to get them to purchase anything but to get them to the point of consideration: "it's a light, early awareness from which additional steps would be necessary to generate revenue for a company."

CONAGRA

As mentioned, Heather Dumford works for ConAgra Foods, one of North America's largest food companies: its brands include Hebrew National (hot dogs), Gulden's (mustard), Hunt's (tomato sauce), Chef Boyardee (pasta), Peter Pan (peanut butter), Pam (cooking spray), Orville Redenbacher (popcorn), and Healthy Choice (meals), to name just a few. Because ConAgra has so many brands, Dumford said the company has "ramped up and focused heavily on native" for some, while "others still use it sparingly."

One ConAgra brand that does a lot of native advertising is Slim Jim, whose primary target market is young men (even if many other demographics eat and enjoy Slim Jims). According to Dumford, because young men frequent websites that "solely rely on native placements," ConAgra's advertising strategy is "to entertain that consumer as opposed to interrupt them"; therefore, native advertising for this brand is "an all-in strategy." In fact, she says ConAgra no longer uses banner ads—at least, not for Slim Jim—unless they are part of a native advertising package. Most of the platforms on which these native ads appear focus primarily on millennials.

For example, ConAgra partnered with Funny Or Die (the comedy website cofounded by Will Ferrell) and created a series of native videos that are not pre-roll commercials or mid-roll ads; instead, they were created as actual entertaining content that consumers would actively want to watch. You can find these on funnyordie.com/slimjim: there is a series of 90-second videos that feature "Greg the Genie" who appears in a cloud of smoke when someone bites into a Slim Jim and makes a wish. One video shows a frustrated guy trying to put together a bookcase who takes a bite of his Slim Jim and wishes that it could be built already so he could go have a beer. Greg the Genie shows up, conjures up two scary-looking tough guys who put together the bookcase, then hands a beer to the guy who made the wish. In another, a guy bites into his Slim Jim and wishes he could be at a barbecue instead of mowing his lawn; Greg the Genie shows up and conjures three Polish women cooking kielbasa and pierogis, with a goat to eat the lawn. These videos may not be laugh-out-loud uproarious, but they are silly and diverting. In addition, they all feature a "partner" banner at the beginning, to clarify that they are sponsored ads that are funded by Slim Jim as a brand partner.

ConAgra has dabbled with native advertising for all its brands, though Dumford said that the company has done it more with some brands than others. Also, she points out that the extent of ConAgra's native advertising depends on how one defines "native": many people consider any advertising that appears on social platforms as being native, and all of ConAgra's brands are fairly active on platforms like Facebook. For example, Marie Callender's has its own Facebook page that fans of the brand can follow (Figure 6.1).

FIGURE 6.1 Marie Callender's Facebook post

ConAgra brands are also showcased on Pinterest, just like other pins from a format standpoint, as you can see in Figure 6.2

for Marie Callender's. ConAgra's marketing department works across every brand within its portfolio, with a very small internal team of just a few people. This team works with an outside agency (comprising approximately 20 people) that does consumer analysis and then helps the company determine how to best spend its advertising dollars. A separate agency comes up with the creative concepts, although sometimes a platform will suggest an idea—for example, Funny Or Die came up with the idea for Greg the Genie for the Slim Jim videos. In general, however, ConAgra briefs its media partner by sharing what it's trying to achieve, then the agency comes up with content ideas.

FIGURE 6.2 Marie Callender's pins on Pinterest

Overall, ConAgra is pleased with the native advertising that's been done for its various brands. The company measures the impact in whatever ways it can, although Dumford admits it's a little difficult to measure the impact of each view. For something like the Greg the Genie ads for Slim Jim that appeared on Funny Or Die, ConAgra has surveyed thousands of people who have seen the videos to determine their perception of the Slim Jim brand; it then compared that perception against that of people who have not seen any. Based on the difference in perception, ConAgra deemed that campaign successful. The company even saw an uptick in sales, which it attributes to this ad campaign by using a sophisticated analysis that excluded price changes, competition, and other factors so it could isolate the effect of this particular advertising campaign. As Dumford summed up, "Overall, native definitely helps to drive sales."

INTEL

At Intel, Luke Kintigh said his company works with all the major native advertising vendors (Outbrain, Taboola, Sharethrough, etc.) on in-feed recommendations, but it also uses a more sophisticated approach to native advertising, which involves different KPIs based on the particular native advertising partner. As of 2016, approximately 80 percent of Intel's native advertising budget is spent on amplifying the company's own content, rather than working with, say BuzzFeed on a specific campaign, although Kintigh said that BuzzFeed is probably the number one publisher Intel has worked with for the previous two to three years. Intel has created videos and quizzes about a variety of different products, which have run mostly on BuzzFeed but also on Mashable, Quartz, and Business Insider.

According to Kintigh, Intel aired several videos on its half-tablet/half-laptop on BuzzFeed. People respond favorably to this type of native advertising because they're getting value from this content, in contrast to what they deem to be annoying pop-ups or banner ads that they don't even look at before closing them.

Intel focused primarily on attitudinal KPIs, measuring the perception of Intel as a brand. Intel developed different brand survey questions to measure the effectiveness of content; secondarily, it also measured more typical factors, including the cost per engagement, click-through rates, first-click performance, scroll rate, and time on site. The goal is to determine whether these ads contribute to or affect brand lift or purchase intent—in other words, whether consumers are more likely to purchase an Intel product based on what they've just engaged with.

Kintigh said the percent of Intel's total marketing/advertising budget that's devoted to native advertising is "still pretty small . . . [only] about three to four percent of our total budget." Nevertheless, it's "definitely" successful. To Intel, native advertising depends fundamentally on the function and the format; it's not just a new ad unit. For native to be successful, a brand needs to put the right content and the right creative inside the unit. Kintigh believes some advertisers think they can simply take exactly what was created for a banner ad and move that into a native ad; unfortunately, that doesn't really work.

Intel has considerable success with the content it develops for its own digital magazine and media property, IQ.Intel.com (which I first described in Chapter 2). Kintigh attributes this success to the fact that the magazine is editorially driven, puts its audience first, and can therefore compete with editorial content from commercial publishers. As he said, IQ.Intel.com is "built for in-feed native advertising where it's not overt marketing. It's not a sales-first message. It's interesting, compelling content that can live underneath a Forbes article or above something from CNN and can be just as interesting to the consumer."

The structure of IQ.Intel.com is similar to a traditional newsroom, with about eight different departments focused on subject matter that will appeal to the IQ audience—from gaming (which is, not surprisingly, a very engaged audience) to fashion (which caters to a very young, female audience and tends to focus on how technology is influencing the future of fashion). The content ranges from trend reports to practical information and includes both how-to content and entertainment-driven content. The editorial team is small, typically only three in-house Intel employees who write much of the content and also edit the work of an external network of about 15 writers who contribute fairly regularly. Intel typically publishes 35 to 40 posts a month on IQ, and much of the content is long-form, more than 1,000 words per article. The goal is to publish fewer pieces than previously but to make those articles higher quality, as well as accompanied by videos and other visual elements.

About 65 percent of the audience of IQ is millennial, although that can vary depending on the topic—for instance, gaming also attracts 35- to 50-year old men. In contrast, the fashion segment attracts women ages 18 to 24, and the content for fashion is very short-form and much more visual. Intel has also been successful in distributing its short-form fashion content on Instagram; Kintigh said Intel's distribution channels vary based on the audience vertical. Finally, about half the audience is from the United States, the other half is international, and 70 to 75 percent of the traffic comes via mobile devices.

Kintigh thinks Intel's native advertising will increase, as the company develops more content that's built for native ad placement and the native environment. Currently, Intel is trying to build an audience on IQ.Intel.com, to get people to engage with the content so that they'll come back to the site and sign up for e-mail updates, because the goal is to build a subscription strategy and e-mail database.

Kintigh mentioned a few other brands he thinks are doing innovative work in native advertising. The first was GE, which so many other people have also cited as at the forefront of innovation: GE is doing everything from virtual reality to podcasts and is continually testing new spaces and new ad products. Kintigh also cited Kraft as having a very robust digital magazine (similar to Intel's IQ, though obviously with very different content). He feels Kraft is doing a good job of publishing "Food and Family" content that's driven by recipes, and then distributing that in the right places through native ad formats. "They're not as sexy as Red Bull, but what they're doing with their "Food and Family" is pretty awesome."

Finally, as a consumer, he engages with a lot of native advertising. Whenever he browses Twitter, Facebook, Flipboard, or any other site where he consumes content, he also sees native ads, and he said he often clicks on them simply because they are interesting and compelling: "I consume a lot of native content naturally, because it's served up in a way that's relevant to the experience in the format I'm looking for." One example he mentioned is the virtual reality program that GE produced with the *New York Times*:

he said he had just purchased Google Cardboard when he discovered GE's take on the future of the industrial revolution. "It was awesome," he noted, adding "Now that I've tested out other formats within virtual reality using Google Cardboard, it's probably one of the best examples of virtual reality I've consumed.

QUALCOMM

Liya Sharif said Qualcomm is also working to build its brand, though not for a general consumer audience. Instead, she says, "We're targeting more technology leaders and tech enthusiasts for Qualcomm corporate brand work, and as part of that, we are using native advertising to really deepen understanding of what Qualcomm is. . . . We license technology that will connect the future of the Internet, the billions of devices that will become connected and intelligent and talk to one another." Native advertising is helping Qualcomm become better known: "It allows us to expand our storytelling; it provides longer-form content opportunities; and it also is the format within publishers and targets where we want people to see us. It's a deeper storytelling opportunity for our brand."

For example, Qualcomm worked with the *Atlantic*'s creative marketing group, Atlantic Re:think, to create a project called "Could: Painting What's Possible." This project showcased the work of an oil painter, a paper sculptor, and an illustrator to demonstrate the future possibilities of technology. Qualcomm wanted to establish itself as a thought leader through the artistic depiction of technology.

The company also works with Quartz (which is also part of Atlantic Media) to develop native advertising programs that are sponsored but also very topical and thematic, on the future of innovation. And it works with the *Huffington Post* on some native placements. In addition, Qualcomm has used a more programmatic approach to native advertising, by creating in-depth essays on various topics, which the company then distributes via Outbrain across the web and to select publishers. Another site the company uses is CNET.

To create its native ads, Qualcomm works in one of three ways. One way is for a publisher to generate the content. So many publishers have their own custom branded content creators, so it's easy for Qualcomm to collaborate with those teams to choose a topic and the direction of a native ad. Then, the publisher's branded content team creates the ad, whether it's a written piece or a video. Qualcomm reviews the piece, approves it, and then lets it go live. The second way native ads are generated is by an agency that is an extension of the company's branded content team. The agency helps craft a series of articles or a video on a particular topic, and then Qualcomm distributes that content via a publisher—for example, Quartz. In those cases, the publisher reviews the content that Qualcomm has created. Finally, the third way is for Qualcomm to generate content in house, which it can do because it has so many employees who are subject matter experts. Which approach the company uses depends on each particular project, but all are part of Qualcomm's native advertising program.

Qualcomm wouldn't divulge what percent of its marketing and advertising budget is devoted to native advertising. Sharif did say it's growing, as part of the company's larger branding efforts and media strategy.

ZENITH

When determining what percentage of marketing or advertising should be devoted to native as opposed to traditional print or TV, Jeff Ratner said Zenith typically takes a zero-based approach and considers the scale of the opportunity and how important each audience is to that particular brand. Native often has production charges that are different from traditional media placement. According to Ratner, "The tug of war these days is between native and social, and while native had been growing, a lot of that now is moving over to social."

Although some people consider native advertising and advertising on social media to be interchangeable, Ratner explains that *native* generally appears in content environments (for example, with a premium publisher or in a very content-specific space), whereas *social* appears (naturally) within social channels, such as Facebook or Twitter. However, Ratner suggested that the explosion of social inventory, the ability to buy it programmatically, and the strong ROI from social is starting to move native more to social media and social content.

Ratner called BuzzFeed "the poster child of native" because it does so much of it, especially in the format of the listicles already discussed. Some of them are quite good, but there are also some misses among the hits, though Ratner didn't cite any in particular. Zenith typically includes BuzzFeed (and other platforms) on the brief for its clients, and then they come back with a few ideas. Finally, when asked if he had ever seen a piece of content that he didn't realize was advertising at first, he said no: "My antenna is up pretty sharp on that."

MORE ON GE

Adam Shlachter is president of VM1, a dedicated full-service media agency for Verizon, as part of Zenith. The agency provides and manages a multitude of media services for clients, including strategy and insights in planning; media buying and delivery across channels; and measurement, optimization, and analysis of the forms and how all the advertising works together. According to Shlachter, "The trick is, it's not 'one size fits all.'" As a result, native advertising has been difficult to scale, which therefore presents the challenge of having to produce many different native ads to suit each different forum. Also, it's critical for the brand message to enhance value for the audience, so that people will want to spend the time reading or viewing it; otherwise, as Shlachter points out, "you just create noise, and you don't actually enrich anyone's experience." Obviously, that's *not* what any company wants to do.

Like many others, Shlachter cited GE's work in native advertising: he thinks the company has taken out a lot of the complexity of what it does through engineering and innovation and distilled that down to some of the amazing things GE made possible. He mentioned the GE "imagination" ads; the editorial content GE has created on BuzzFeed, Quartz, and other platforms; and the commissioning of feature-length television programming with Ron Howard for National Geographic's NatGeo TV channel.

GE has partnered with the *Economist* magazine on articles about the future of technology in many fields, under the byline "GE Look Ahead." For example, consider an article entitled "What if we could live for 120 years?" with the subtitle, "extreme longevity is increasingly possible. With it will come major societal shifts." This article was posted under the GE byline on the *Economist*'s site on January 21, 2016, and although it's rather brief, it does offer statistics about longevity as well as commentary from credentialed experts in healthcare, finance (which will naturally be a concern, if people live longer), and other areas. In other words, it reads like a journalist researched this topic, interviewed experts, and wrote a factual account about changes in longevity trends, and it *doesn't* read like a pitch for GE products or technologies.

Jason Hill, GE's director of global media strategy made it clear that all of these articles are written in a journalistic way by a GE editorial team, which develops content that moves "from advertising to storytelling," in Hill's words.[6] He went on to say that media outlets are starting to pick up GE's stories "the way they could syndicate from a press outlet." One reason for this is the decline of local newspapers in many cities and towns; without those journalists, there's a gap in information, and if GE (and other companies) can provide it, so much the better. Hill says the GE writers operate as though they're working in a traditional newsroom, but The Media Briefing points out that this content "is at least partially in service of the GE brand." Such is the case with native advertising.

The TV show that Shlachter referred to is called *Breakthrough* and was developed by actor/director Ron Howard and TV and film producer Brian Grazer of Imagine Entertainment. *Breakthrough* is a documentary series of six episodes describing scientific innovations in such topics as alternative energies, water conservation, the human brain, fighting pandemics, what it means to be human, and aging. The shows feature scientists who work for or with GE,[7] but like the print work GE is doing, the focus is on the science, not on GE products. According to the *New York Times*, the company's goal for the series "was not to sell more light bulbs or other GE products, but to spread awareness about the company's contributions to science and technology."[8] The company helped choose the topics that would be presented in each show, and it gave the producers access to GE research centers to facilitate story ideas.

Courteney Monroe, Chief Executive of National Geographic Channels U.S., said GE's partnership with NatGeo presented a way for the network to align itself with a company beyond traditional sponsorship. In other words, although companies still spend billions on TV commercials, TV networks also need to adapt to different ways of working with brands. Regarding the possibility that viewers might not realize GE's connection to the show, she said, "I don't think it has to be plastered all over the screen, [but] we'll make sure that everyone knows that GE has been part of it." When asked if viewers still may not realize that this is native advertising, she conceded that "it's a risk, [but] good content has to be risky."[9]

GE also created a recurring segment on NBC's *The Tonight Show*: in early 2014, Jimmy Fallon started featuring "GE's Fallonvention," which showcased gadgets invented by teenagers, such as a flashlight that is powered by the heat from a person's hand. According to Linda Boff, who was then-executive director of global brand marketing and was appointed GE's CMO in 2015, General Electric first embraced native advertising as early as 2010, doing in-stream advertising with BuzzFeed and Tumblr.

She said the Fallonvention idea was a "home run" for the company: the first segment was watched 333,106 times on YouTube, with a video completion rate of 92 percent .[10]

In all these media, Shlachter said, GE tells "rich and amazing stories" about all the products and innovations and technologies that GE helped propel, create, built, or develop. Shlachter thinks GE has "done a really fascinating job" with its native advertising; in fact, riffing on the company's slogan ("we bring good things to life"), he feels GE has executed "some really clever integrations to bring the brand to life."

L'ORÉAL AND JARDEN

Shlachter also cited L'Oréal as a brand that has done native advertising successfully. Several years ago, the brand commissioned beauty bloggers to create editorial for L'Oréal. The result was really rich, easily accessible video content that didn't appear in the pages of *Vogue*, for example; instead, it was presented *by* millennial women via their blogs and on platforms like YouTube, *for* millennial women who were looking for beauty tips.

Another company he thinks is doing interesting work is Jarden (which was acquired in 2016 by Newell Rubbermaid and renamed Newell Brands). Before being acquired itself, Jarden had previously bought various consumer-products brands, including Coleman, Mr. Coffee, Crockpot, Sunbeam, and many others. Shlachter cited videos that Jarden developed with Buzz-Feed and posted on Facebook to show how to make easy one-pot recipes, for example, in a Crockpot. The videos use time-lapsing to show how, in 90 seconds or so, viewers can use their product to make a 30-minute or even a three-hour-long meal. The videos break down the recipes into very simple steps, to demonstrate the value of using the company's products and to show how they can simplify your life by making really good food really easily.

Shlachter says these videos have had "insane virality" because the video developers have figured out what people want to watch—and share—in their feeds. People want to see something they think of as complex being simplified, and if it's a company's product that shows how easy it is to use to accomplish that, so be it. The videos also have to be mobile-friendly because that's how people are viewing them: they need to fit into viewers' feeds so they can consume them in these "snackable" ways, so that viewers can then repost or share or comment on or make their own. The brands that are being promoted receive another benefit in that they get great feedback from viewers.

One disadvantage of using this type of format is that it's easily imitated. And although imitation is the sincerest form of flattery (as the old saying goes), too much imitation also makes the Internet noisier and more "cluttered," as Shlachter said, which is why "it's great to be the brand that breaks the mold and creates [something new, and] it's tough to be the brand that says, *oh, I want one of those*, because then the uniqueness is diluted, and it becomes less of [a] native form of advertising [and] just another form of commercial advertising." Shlachter believes (as many others do) that the essence of native ads are that they fit in and are unique to the environment that features them. When that's the case, the native ads fit in, and the brands and advertisers are making the best use of the opportunity to make an actual impression, rather than just cutting down a 30-second ad and then slapping it in front of a piece of content that's only 90 seconds long and doesn't actually fit that environment or platform at all.

eBAY

Rebecca Babcock described eBay's innovative branded content platform that invites premium publishing partners to create content for the site. These partners have a large engaged audience—for example, a blogger who has attracted many readers on his or her specific topic. Here's how she describes what eBay is currently doing:

> We have an internal CMS at eBay that creates content in the form of guides for us. They're not what you might think: they're not necessarily selling products, although obviously the guides have product aligned with it; [instead,] it's more an upper-funnel-awareness play. It's really more about generating awareness with the Refinery29 audience, or the PureWow audience, or the Thrillist audience, or Vox Media, or whatever audience [is being targeted. The goal is to] generate awareness for eBay and create an *a-ha* moment. So it's less about buy X or Y from eBay . . . and more the storytelling behind it.

For example, Babcock mentions that PureWow developed a guide on the must-have wearable technology right now, technology that is both attractive and fashionable as well as useful—"the Tory Burch version of Fitbit."

Babcock says her role is to find publishing platforms for these guides; when she started, there were only three, whereas at the time she was interviewed for this book, there were 18. She helps eBay identify who would be the right partner for a particular category of products, and then she helps the publishers develop themes for the guides they're going to write that will resonate with their specific audience. In addition, eBay has an internal team of people who write guides based on what eBay already knows are its popular products within the eBay audience, from people who are already buying on eBay. Babcock's goal is to bring a *new* audience in, to find out what the audience of each publishing platform is most interested in, what that audience loves and gets excited about.

Then that publisher writes a guide about those topics, which appears not on the publisher's platform, but on the eBay site. The publisher will promote it on its own homepage, on social media with dedicated e-mail blasts, and with various other tactics. However, eBay is the only place that readers will be able to get the full information provided in that particular guide. According to Babcock, there are thousands of guides on eBay. But the publisher that writes the guide is solely responsible for driving traffic to that guide, because eBay's algorithm is set up so that when someone searches for something on eBay, that search is going to lead to something that's for sale, not to a guide. That's why it's up to eBay's publishing partners to come up with the promotional tactics to drive the traffic to their guides on eBay.

Babcock said eBay is extremely proud of this program, and she thinks it's very innovative for such a large company to be doing this type of branded content. Babcock works directly with the publishers, suggesting general topics to them that will be relevant for different times of the year—for example, summer content will differ from fall content, which is oriented more to back-to-school topics. But the publishers originate the ideas for the specific content, then Babcock approves the idea and then reviews the content before it goes live on eBay's site. She has the authority to accept or reject a guide, which she has done on occasion, because obviously, eBay is paying the publishers for this type of branded content/native advertising, so it has the final word on what works. But as Babcock summed up, if you "start with what your reader is interested in, and because pretty much anything on the planet earth is for sale on eBay you're going to be able to find something to fit your theme."

MICROSOFT

Hilary Batsel at Microsoft says her company also reposts third-party material about the company and its products, but more of its efforts are devoted to creating its own material. The third-party material "provides an additional source of credibility" because it's created by someone other than a Microsoft employee. When Microsoft develops its own native advertising, that content has typically been stories of "how technology has empowered individuals to better improve the planet."

Batsel offers an example of Microsoft producing a content piece about bringing Internet opportunities to a country in Africa that had not had those opportunities before. The targeted readers for such a story would likely be individuals who have an entrepreneurial spirit and are interested in growing developing nations around the world, so then the company needs to find publishing opportunities where they can surround relevant content, for example, a site that features other stories about similar humanitarian efforts, because that's where there will be an audience that's most likely receptive to this type of native advertising. Batsel says this is a real example, although it's not live currently.

Batsel said Microsoft doesn't break out what percentage of its marketing is devoted to native advertising vs. traditional print or TV; the company simply views native advertising as part of its overall digital plan.

She admitted that Microsoft probably did less native advertising than many other brands at the time, and she attributed that to the fact that the company is very selective in this type of marketing and advertising. As she put it: "We don't see it as necessarily an opportunity for a large scale, because we want to make sure we have more of a one-to-one conversation and that the contextual relevancy is there [instead of] just pushing out our advertisement."

She also conceded that it may be the technology industry as a whole (and not only Microsoft in particular) that is doing less native advertising than, for instance, the packaged goods industry. She cited Pepsi as one example of a brand that has many different initiatives that it's working on, in terms of native content (although this is simply her opinion, based on observation; Batsel has never worked for Pepsi). When I looked into this further, I found a fascinating example of a TV commercial that wasn't shown as a commercial but was embedded into the story line of the TV show *Empire*, where one of the characters creates an ad for Pepsi and then shows it in its entirety. That's brilliant! As Seth Kaufman, Pepsi's CMO, said, "This idea of being native, whatever the context, is so powerful. Here you have *Empire* viewers and anyone who engages with the show or its social platforms seeing

Pepsi in a truly authentic and contextually powerful advertising strategy. This to me is exactly what native is."[11]

Batsel reminds us, though, that packaged goods (such as Pepsi) may have more and better opportunities to do this type of native advertising because it's focused more on entertainment. In contrast, "If you're producing a lot of content that needs explanation, like how to use a product, that then becomes more educational and less entertainment, and you don't necessarily put that in native advertising as much." That's another reason why Microsoft is very selective about when to use native advertising versus other forms of advertising and marketing.

In terms of how Microsoft chooses which digital publications for native advertising, that depends, of course, on what demographic the company is targeting. As she described, "It's all about the consumer . . . [and] with our consumer audiences, we always look at where they are spending their time . . . should we be looking at TV vs. digital vs. print." Microsoft also considers what partner best suits each demographic: "Within each of the categories, are they consuming more news information or less news information? More style information? What are their passions that they're really spending time on? Then where are the sites or the partners they're going to as their source of information?"

For example, she mentioned that the Windows and Surface brands have many similarities, but they have different audiences. And although both audiences might like style, "the Surface audience is a little bit more trendy" so Microsoft might do native ads for it on a site like Refinery29—a website that defines itself as "the modern woman's destination for how to live a stylish, well-rounded life"—whereas the Windows audiences are also interested in style, but they're more likely to go to sites that offer other types of information as well—for example, the *Washington Post*.

When asked which companies besides Microsoft that she thinks are doing interesting native advertising campaigns, Batsel mentioned Intel, especially a "unique" innovation series that Intel has been promoting and which she thinks culminated with Lady Gaga's performance at the 2016 Grammys. After she mentioned this, I discovered that Intel had indeed executed some amazing technologies, including creating "digital skin"—actually an animated face for the singer, which enabled her to change her appearance during a single performance. Intel also provided interactive video so that Lady Gaga could control how she appeared against an LED wall; robotics that enabled her piano to appear to dance; and interactive holograms that created a three-dimensional version of Gaga.[12] Batsel's point, though, was not so much about the initial TV performance at the Grammys but about the fact that Intel was able to continue to promote these technologies via native advertising on other media besides TV, revealing the backstories about how that performance was developed. As she described it: Intel has "found interesting ways to push out that information from the angle at which that consumer would be interested, either a tech angle or a music angle to reach a broader audience and still make it relevant." Which is, after all, the goal of effective native advertising.

Finally, Microsoft identifies all of its native advertising by indicating that it is paid advertising. This is true of both the company's own first-party messaging (content it creates itself); as well as third-party editorial pieces that Microsoft is promoting on its site; and even promotions from influencers that the company has worked with and paid money to support (for example, via tweet). All of these indicate that they are paid ads, to ensure transparency and to reassure consumers will know exactly where these messages are coming from.

NATIVE ADVERTISING IN PRINT PUBLICATIONS

As I've mentioned several times so far, not all native advertising is digital. Cadillac is one brand that cited an example of native advertising that it created for a print publication—namely, *Esquire*.[13] Cadillac, of course, works with many publishers whose readership matches the target demographic of the Cadillac brand. This particular campaign was done in conjunction with a 10-page "Men of Style" photo shoot that appeared in *Esquire*'s September 2015 issue. And while native advertising was the centerpiece, Cadillac took a multifaceted approach leveraging PR, social, and experiential to bring the campaign to consumers. In the *Esquire* spread, a gorgeous new Cadillac appeared in every page of the fashion shoot, with almost as much emphasis on the car as on the fashions of each man walking in front of each car. The campaign was shot mostly on the streets of New York City, in black and white, and profiled the men wearing the fashions. To launch, Cadillac hosted an event that was part of New York's Fashion Week in July 2016, where the clothing featured in the shoot was shown prior to being available for purchase via Gilt. But the Cadillac campaign was a paid engagement with *Esquire* that spanned the print publication and a website. Figure 6.3 shows a sample:

FIGURE 6.3 Cadillac's "Men of Style" partnership with *Esquire*

Eric Jillard, director of brand execution at Cadillac, pointed out that this isn't so far away from print native advertising of yesteryear, where magazines featured what they called "special advertising sections" that were pages of paid ads that were made to look like editorial but weren't. These special ad sections were inserted between pages of the magazine, so page 53, for example, would be followed by an ad insert, and then by page 54. In this case—the "Men of Style" photo shoot—Cadillac created this campaign in partnership with *Esquire*.

Cadillac is also working on a campaign for its new CT6 model with the *Washington Post*'s WP Brand Studio (which is the *Post*'s native advertising department, similar to the *New York Times*' T Brand Studio). Readers of the *Washington Post* are a strong demographic fit for Cadillac. For this campaign, the marketing team at Cadillac briefed the staff of the WP Brand Studio on the key features and desirable attributes of this new model of Cadillac, and the campaign that grew out of that brief is called "Strong and Silent." The focus of the content, according to Jillard, is the power of silence in negotiations, how quiet manifests itself in business and politics and other behind-the-scenes negotiations between decision-makers.

Jillard explains that this is "clearly sponsored by Cadillac but is, in all respects, legitimate editorial content." In addition, the content doesn't talk about cars at all, because in an article about the power of silence in negotiations, "there really isn't an obvious way to bring in the car in a way that feels organic to the piece." The content will be accompanied by Cadillac advertising, so the intent is to subtly link, in readers' minds, the connection between quiet and power in negotiations with silence and power in the new Cadillac models.

As discussed throughout this book, ideas for native advertising come from a variety of sources. Sometimes the brand itself comes up with the idea; other times, the brand's ad agency comes up with the idea. And sometimes the publishers that want to feature native advertising come up with the idea. Jillard explained that Cadillac will consider the unique selling propositions (USPs) of its vehicles, then brief several relevant publishers and let them know they're looking for campaign ideas for a particular vehicle.

That's how the *Washington Post* Cadillac native ads came to be: after the initial briefing, WP Brand Studio came back to Cadillac and noted how quiet the vehicle was, even with the new three-liter twin-turbo engine, and said: "We thought this juxtaposition of quiet, but powerful, was an interesting idea. So we'd like to pitch you on an idea that leans into [how] often the power in a situation is very quiet. And here's the concept." Cadillac agreed, and that's how the campaign developed.

Cadillac also promotes third-party content with companies like Outbrain and Sharethrough. The Cadillac brand has suffered in recent years, ironically, because of its success in the past. It has a long history, but that translates into the average buyer being 59 years old. It's number four in the luxury car segment, behind BMW, Mercedes, and Lexus, from a sales perspective.[14] Jillard described the brand's challenges by saying, "Some of the people in our target audience have a very nostalgic view of Cadillac. This is partly because those who hold the current buying power in the luxury segment grew up with the brand, so they may shy away because it is what their parents drove. Our challenge is to break that false familiarity and get the message out that Cadillacs like ATS-V, for example—a car that is sportier than the equivalent BMW—might beat an M3 in a head-to-head test. We need people to be exposed to that content, so we have definitely leaned into promoted content, and we see results that say it does lift brand familiarity, brand favorability, intention to consider."

Jillard said he likes the idea of sponsored content, though he conceded that "it's not for everybody." But with Cadillac, the company is trying to surprise people, so it's eager for its target market to see a teaser like, *Which car just beat the BMW M3 in a head-to-head test?* If you clicked on that, it would lead you to an actual article—"pure editorial content" that was *not* written by Cadillac—from *Motor Trend* magazine. The article compares the Cadillac ATS-V with the BMW M3 and the Mercedes-AMG C63S, and it reveals that the Cadillac "hits 60 mph in a remarkable 3.7 seconds. That's as quick as a Corvette Sting-ray . . . and quicker than a Camaro Z/28 . . . The conclusion from our test team is that if performance is all you care about, buy the Cadillac."[15]

Jillard says Cadillac is "convinced" that this type of advertising "is working very hard for us now." He recognizes that it's not the type of advertisement that's going to lead *directly* or immediately to sales, but he believes it's a great way to get people thinking about Cadillac in a new way. It's the type of ad that a reader is very likely to forward to friends, which also helps get the word out. The company also uses other articles that tout the Cadillac as a great car: Jillard proudly notes that the Cadillac CTS has been on the *Car & Driver* "10 best list" for the third year in a row, that combats the perception that Cadillac does not make driver-focused cars. As Jillard summed up, "Our cars are so well-acclaimed critically that there is an opportunity to cash in on that from a sales perspective, given how good they are," which is why the company is committed to doing more sponsored content, because "people don't want to hear what we say about our own cars, but they want to hear what other people say about our cars."

Also, it's not only the cars themselves that Cadillac promotes through native advertising; it also promotes the technologies that are features of its vehicles. For example, Jillard mentioned a campaign the company was working on, for the CT6, with the news site Quartz (QZ.com). The article was sponsored content about how technology is changing the way people live—for example, via devices for the home that respond to voice commands, home security smart devices, public Wi-Fi that facilitates education—and, of course, new technologies in the Cadillac CT6, such as enhanced night vision that uses heat sensors to detect animals and people on the road that drivers might not otherwise see.[16]

Finally, Jillard pointed out that it's not only the car industry that is doing more sponsored content and native advertising. We've seen this throughout this chapter, but perhaps Jillard said it best: "I think all marketers are struggling with the same overall trends, and . . . everybody's looking to figure out how to do native in a way that achieves the relevance and the engagement that they're looking for. I think everybody's trying to figure out how to do this right." The examples in this chapter showcase pioneering efforts by advertisers that are collaborating with publishers to create branded content experiences for readers that inform consumers.

CHAPTER 7

CONSUMER REACTION

Not surprisingly, most people prefer to read ads that don't look like ads: one study found that 25 percent more consumers looked at sponsored articles than display ads.[1] Another study claims that 95 percent of the time, websites that feature branded content were more successful than websites featuring typical advertisements—and are 24 percent more effective at increasing the purchase intent of viewers.[2] Finally, more consumers are shifting their web consumption to mobile devices, where sponsored content is believed to have more impact than standard banner ads.[3] This chapter looks at how consumers feel about this latest type of advertising.

One publisher said he hasn't gotten much pushback from consumers against native advertising: "There's occasionally grumbling about *what is this crap?* when a brand published something that was kind of crap, but I also hear that grumbling when journalists publish listicles and things that are crap. Good is good, and crap is crap, regardless of the source."

Another publisher said he has never heard from any consumer that it was difficult to tell what is editorial content written by journalists and what is native advertising written by marketing or advertising people. He said journalists are the only ones who believe it's difficult to tell the difference.

A third publisher elaborated further: "I think consumers care about, *Is the content good? Have you disclosed your relationship with the advertiser? Is it useful and entertaining and good for me?*" He emphasized that the publications he oversees have no interest in (or benefit from) misleading readers about their relationships with their advertisers. Their goal is not to sell overt product endorsements, nor do they deliver hard news, but he conceded that publications that are in those businesses would likely have a different set of concerns regarding their consumers.

When he reads other publications as a consumer, if he comes across a piece of native advertising that he finds objectionable, he simply skips it. He believes this is what most consumers do: they have the power to either engage or not engage because they are more aware and savvier than many people give them credit for being: "We live in a highly commercial world, and [consumers] have so many choices . . . and a lot of opportunities to make decisions" about what they choose to read or view. He does concede that consumers "have a right to be concerned" if they feel they are "being hoodwinked" by content that purports to be unbiased but is actually a paid advertisement or endorsement of a product.

Yet another publisher said he "almost never" gets negative reactions from subscribers or readers. He attributes that to the fact that native ads, by their very nature, are nonintrusive, which was certainly *not* the case during "the first 15 years of digital advertising, [which featured] pop-up windows and push-down ads and the robot walking across the screen—all those intrusive executions."

He also compared the early years of digital publishing to the heyday of print magazines, especially lifestyle magazines (such as *ELLE, Harper's Bazaar,* and other fashion magazines), where the advertising in those publications actually "*added* to the value of the reader experience. There's a reason why people love the September issue of *ELLE* more than the August issue of *ELLE*. Why?

Because it has five times as much advertising, and advertising adds to the reader experience. In the first 15 years of the web, that was not the case, because it was all intrusive advertising."[4]

In contrast, branded content delivers advertising messages in a nonintrusive way, by matching the tone and the voice of the brand, while being transparent so readers know this is being brought to them in collaboration with an advertiser. As a result, Todd Haskell considers this "the holy grail of what we can do for an advertiser and for the reader, and is why when done well, we don't get complaints about it." With this type of advertising, consumers are much more likely to accept content that *House Beautiful*, for example, created with Behr paint that discusses trends in color and how to choose a color for one's own house, in contrast to the type of intrusive ads that typically appeared not so long ago, which featured "an animated dude walking across the page splashing paint on the home page in order to get your attention."

Adam Kasper at Havas agreed that most consumers are not as concerned about native advertising as we might think they are. Instead, he believes that "people get more freaked out when we talk about consumer behavior, mobile tracking technologies, and . . . privacy." He concurred with others interviewed for this book that consumers are savvy enough to understand that companies pay to promote their products and that native advertising is not much different from, for example, Macy's featuring a particular designer's fashions in its display windows because that designer paid for that promotion.

Meredith Levien described some of the initial concerns the *New York Times* had about consumer reaction when it first started doing native advertising. She admitted that when she was appointed EVP in 2013, "it was a scary proposition to be the person who said, 'we're going to launch native advertising on the *New York Times*.' . . . In the beginning, there was a fair amount of worry [about] what would we do to the *Times* brand?"

To counter that uneasiness, the *Times* has been "particularly religious" about striving "to never confuse readers" and, according to Levien, has "taken a more proactive approach to labeling than anybody else in the space," so much so that "we have set a standard for other serious brands" that started doing native advertising after the *Times* established T Brand Studio. The *Times* has also been rigorous about labeling all its native advertising with "paid post" so that it's clear that these pieces are paid for by marketers or brands or advertisers. Levien is confident that it's because of those transparent disclosures that the *Times* doesn't get a lot of negative feedback from readers:

> I wouldn't say there's never a reader complaint, but they're relatively few and far between. . . . We've been really careful about how we've gone about it. There are spaces we don't play in. We definitely won't launch something that we think runs the risk of being confusing or where we don't feel like the creative lives up to a standard. We absolutely don't take every request we get, and I think the long game for the *New York Times* is bigger than branded content and bigger than native advertising. We are attempting to reimagine digital advertising into a much higher value experience for the marketer, for the media company, and for the consumer, who is really the most important person in that equation. We are aspiring to do nothing short of making digital advertising

vastly better than it's ever been, and better than the media that's come before it.

GE's content has won the Grand Prix at the Cannes Lions festival, receiving overwhelming positive feedback from its partnership with the *New York Times*. Like Levien at the *Times*, Alexa Christon at GE attributed this to GE's transparent disclosures: "We're really clear about the author and the source and the co-production. We're never trying to hide anything. Actually, when we work with publishers, we try to make that relationship more explicit than less." As a result, "people are generally excited about the experiences we provide and present, so we hear typically positive feedback."

As one example, she again mentioned the piece (described in Chapter 6) that ran in the *New York Times* that featured Google Cardboard headsets with a video from GE about technology inspired by nature. She said this piece "had overwhelmingly positive feedback."

She also cited the "Fallonvention" segments on *The Tonight Show*, saying that people love them, and she attributes the excitement about these segments and the kids' inventions because they're "not about GE, not about pushing a product." Instead, she believes people like them because GE "created a segment that is exciting and aspirational and really meant to talk to the spirit of science and technology and push people to invent."

Christon attributed the company's success with native advertising to the fact that "We've been doing this for a while, we're pretty advanced in it, so our horizon line is maybe a little bit further out than some other brands. We give ourselves a lot of license to move fast and to move first, and we think this is a really exciting space."

WHAT CONSUMERS DON'T LIKE
ABOUT NATIVE ADVERTISING

I did encounter some consumer frustration with native advertising during the interviews for this book. As mentioned in Chapter 1, I heard from a variety of sources that no one really knows *exactly* what constitutes native advertising—as one interviewee expressed it, there seem to be "different interpretations of native advertising. Is it the embedding of ads that you don't know are ads throughout an article, or is it a public relations piece that's actually sponsored by a third party that looks like a news feature?"

In addition to the fact that the interpretations are still confusing, other aspects of some native advertising were clearly frustrating. For example, one person mentioned the constant intrusion of ads that interrupt a piece whenever he's trying to read something. He cited a fictitious example of an article that is the type of piece that would attract his attention while looking at Facebook or BuzzFeed or TipHero or any other online source of info and news:

5 Easy Tips to Financial Security

That's so alluring, right? Everyone wants to be financially secure, and if it's possible to achieve that piece of mind (and wallet) in just *five* simple ways, then sign me up! That type of headline is, of course, *intended* to lure in readers. Unfortunately, once you click on the article and start reading, you won't get very far before you're barraged with advertising that quickly gets in the way of your ability to simply finish this article and find out all five easy tips. As this consumer described this frustrating experience:

You get two lines of copy that's related to what you're looking for, then as you try to scroll down, on your mobile phone, there's an ad, and then another ad. You can't even scroll on your phone without clicking and getting moved to different locations, off the subject you wanted to read about, because you're being fooled by the placement of ads throughout, and they're highly clickable, so you end up going to third parties, and the next thing you know you're downloading Candy Crush Saga or something nonsensical that it led you to. That advertising, where there are embedded links throughout an article, is one interpretation of native advertising to me. The user experience of getting the satisfaction of finding what you're looking for is awful; instead, it's a very distracting and fragmented experience.

WHAT CONSUMERS PREFER ABOUT NATIVE ADVERTISING

Not everyone, however, is frustrated by that experience of being interrupted by paid advertisements. Another person interviewed for this book recalled that the Internet's search function was the first organic native opportunity. Nevertheless, when he searched for something and several results popped up, at least one in the list would be marked as an "Ad." Then it was his choice as to whether or not he would decide to click on that and read it. And he didn't find that frustrating because he had the choice to either ignore it or click on it. The ad was just another option of information that he might—or might not—decide to look at.

Finally, many people seem to already be "jaded" by native advertising because they've seen so much of it and are aware when something they read is "sponsored" or not. Still, people seem to feel that, as one person said, native is "definitely a better end experience for the consumer, because it's not as in your face" as other types of advertising were and continue to be. Another person went on to say, "I do like [native advertising, because] it's generally more relevant. Sometimes, I critique all the content, because I know it's sponsored, and it's not an actual true piece of editorial. . . . Coming from the ad world, that's what I'm always thinking of when I'm reading a piece of sponsored content, even though I find it more enjoyable than other formats of advertising. I definitely am a bit more nitpicky in what I find successful and interesting. If it looks too forced, I will be more put off to the piece of content itself."

CHARACTERISTICS OF EFFECTIVE NATIVE ADVERTISING

In terms of what platforms are publishing effective native advertising, one person (who wished to remain anonymous) cited theSkimm.com, which is a daily newsletter that people subscribe to, to keep up on what's happening in the world. (Its tag line is "We read. You skimm.") It's for people who want to be in the know but don't have or want to spend the time reading a daily newspaper (like the *New York Times* or the *Washington Post* or *USA Today* or any other paper), or who don't have the time or inclination to watch CNN or Fox News or any other traditional

TV news program. TheSkimm.com's founders and staff have "gotten a lot of credit for doing native very well, because they're extremely picky about whom they select as advertisers." This person thinks that "when running native advertising, publishers need to be selective and have the ultimate control on what they're writing, because if brands get too involved, it doesn't sound realistic, and it just sounds very forced."

Finally, this person believes the most effective native advertising is useful, provides a service, or offers some entertainment value. However, she has noticed that some brands choose odd publications on which to run their native ads, almost as though they're not considering that platform's readers (or have no idea who those readers are!). For example, if you're reading a hard-news publication, it doesn't make sense to see native ads from fashion companies, because those readers in this context probably could not care less about, for example, how to tie a sarong at the beach.

She believes the entertainment value of native ads is important because they're another way brands are successfully getting their message out there: "Native advertising isn't all about driving clicks to [a] site; it's not meant to necessarily drive traffic. It's great if it does," but that's not the primary purpose of native advertising. She thinks it's "silly when people are expecting eight billion people to click through their native ads when . . . if people are recognizing it and having a favorable brand experience, that's paramount."

She said BuzzFeed does this pretty well with "Tasty" on Buzz-Feed. She enjoys watching these time-lapsed or time-compressed recipe videos, and she noted that they have "pretty much spread like wildfire, [with] a lot of copycats doing these quick-service native tutorial-style videos."

As she summed it up, "native is really the new norm . . . it's great for [companies that want to] keep their brands out there as an option" and to keep those brands at the top of consumers' minds. However, she thinks it's not as likely that native ads are going to *convert* buyers of mainstream products, such as shampoo, where people tend to be loyal to a particular brand. In contrast, she thinks native ads are better for products that are "unique and nifty". For example, if someone is interested in doing really intricate nail art for manicures and there's a particular tool you need to create that effect, then a native ad promoting that product or technique might work really well to induce its viewers to go out and buy that tool. But she also thinks it's important for companies to do native advertising to "keep their brands relevant . . . that should be the goal of most advertisers. If you don't keep up, you're just a flash in the pan, and people forget about you . . . [so] keeping your brand out there and exposed in a meaningful or interesting way is pretty important."

As we can see from this chapter, the different perspectives offered about native advertising are highly varied and reflect a digital media industry in transition.

CHAPTER 8

BEST PRACTICES AND

RECOMMENDATIONS

As mentioned in the Introduction, this book isn't intended to be a "how-to" guide to native advertising. Instead, the goal is to explain what native advertising is; when native advertising started, and how native advertising has grown and developed; identify examples of when native advertising is done well and when it isn't; tell what disclosures are necessary or mandated; report how journalists feel about native advertising; show how various companies have been doing native advertising; and give insight into what consumers think of native ads.

However, in this final chapter, I wrap up our discussion by examining some of the best practices in this new and changing approach to marketing and advertising products and services. I also highlight what some of the people interviewed for this book have identified as the best examples of native advertising and their recommendations and advice for marketers on how to create or improve the native ads they're currently doing as well as where they think the future of native advertising is headed.

SOME WORDS OF CAUTION

Everyone interviewed for this book had suggestions on how to improve native advertising. Before presenting some of those recommendations, however, here are some of their concerns and complaints, in their own words:

From Kate Lewis: "I'm sure that I have, at some point, been bamboozled when reading something sponsored that

wasn't clearly labeled. I think, to me, that's the most important piece of it: you need to be very clear and transparent up
front."

From Charles Dubow: "As a consumer of media, I would
want native advertising to be completely sectioned off, that it
be made very clear that it is, in fact, not content that has been
actually generated by the journalist at that site, and I would
feel annoyed, if not actually outraged, if I felt that something
I was reading was being misrepresented as something that
it was not. . . . I want it corralled off [like an old-fashioned
advertorial], which is basically what this is."

From Adam Shlachter: "Purely aggregating content that is
not bespoke to one's brand is not the best way to produce
native advertising. Just slapping your logo on [content] is
[also] probably not the strongest way to do it."

Here's a summary of recommendations for how to improve native
advertising:

1. Be very clear and transparent up front.
2. Make sure the article doesn't focus only on one brand or
   product, which is too obviously a pitch for that brand or
   product. Instead, the article should offer useful, general
   information that *might include* references to a particular
   product but also describes products from companies other
   than the sponsoring company.

Good native advertising should be written so that readers or viewers or consumers get something out of the piece, other than a pitch for a product they could buy. For example, recall (from Chapter 5) what journalist Elizabeth Hansen said about the article she read on BuzzFeed that was sponsored by 3M's Post-its: that article offered several tips on how to get better organized that had nothing at all to do with Post-its (as well as a few tips that did suggest using Post-it products).

As Hansen recalled, there was a headline at the top of the piece that said something like, "Paid Advertising," although that didn't really even register with her until she reached an organizing tip that described what to do and concluded with a recommendation along the lines of "You can use Post-its for this." She then scrolled back up to the beginning of the article and saw the "Paid Advertising" headline. When she scrolled down to the end of the article, she saw another statement that read "This is brought to you by Post-it®." Since there were disclosures at both the top and the bottom of the article, Hansen felt that more than sufficiently identified the article as native advertising, because the sponsor wasn't hidden or misleading the viewer in any way; instead, the sponsorship was very clearly stated.

In stark contrast was another article (also mentioned in Chapter 5), where every organizing tip concluded with this recommendation: "You can buy this at _____." In terms of best practices, that's definitely *not* how to do native advertising successfully. Instead, that's a surefire way of turning off readers, who will typically abandon an article that features such blatant product promotion.

In contrast to that piece, Troy Young of Hearst Magazines Digital Media points as an example to "a piece of content that was the number one performing piece of branded content on MarieClaire.com for . . . several months. It was branded content on '10 Hairstyles You Can Do in Literally 10 Seconds,' [which was done] in association with a hair product company. We broadened it so it didn't say, *buy this, buy this, buy this*, . . . we landed on the right idea editorially. It was very simple service-based content, but the photography worked, and the idea worked, and it was good. . . . I think that's cool. [The idea] came out of a collaboration between our branded content team and the editors of MarieClaire.com."

BALANCE NATIVE CONTENT
AND DISCLOSURE

From an advertiser's perspective, the issues surrounding native advertising are a bit more complicated. Luke Kintigh of Intel explained the conundrum this way: "It's a fine line, because once you get into overtly . . . disclosing [that something is sponsored], it becomes less native." As an advertiser, he notes, you want the consumer's overall experience to be native; you want to use the same formats the viewer is accustomed to seeing on a publisher's website; you want everything you present to retain the site's branding and tone. On the other hand, he points out, "If you're sticking up logos and disclosures everywhere, [it] disrupts the experience". Nevertheless, he thinks there should be more consistency in how native ads are labeled, how they are called out.

Kintigh uses the example of search advertising—which was one of the very first forms of digital native advertising, and notes that—those ads looked exactly like a natural, organic search result, although they appeared in a different shade or color, along with one word at the top left that disclosed that that particular result is sponsored. In his belief, if the way disclosure is done is consistent, the consumer will rally around the idea of native advertising, but, as he says, "Right now, it's just so disparate in terms of what publishers do, that it's all different; different platforms are disclosing [sponsored ads] in different ways, but if there was a consistent way to do it, . . . that would solve a lot of these problems."

Jeff Sternstein of ad agency Havas Lynx U.S. emphasizes that successful native advertising is all about offering value and credibility to the reader. That, he says, is paramount. Whatever style you use has to convey the message that your priority is serving the viewer and that you are doing it very selflessly, because being sold to is a universal turnoff.

BALANCE JOURNALISM AND NATIVE ADVERTISING

Dan Bigman, publisher at Verse.com with years of experience as a journalist for *Forbes* and the *New York Times*, thinks many (if not all) companies are now really content providers. He believes that's the result of how quickly digital publications and digital advertising have supplanted traditional print publications in the last 15 years or so. He said this is evident simply in hiring trends:

There's been this enormous explosion in the amount of hiring that's gone on out of journalism into public relations and marketing and advertising, and also brands—not so much at agencies, but at brands themselves. People [are] hiring editors [and] experienced writers—not to come in and [write] press releases . . . there was always a revolving door there—but to come in and really think about *how are we going to present what we do in a way that people are actually going to want to consume it, where it adds [value] rather than distracts [from the content], where it's compelling [and not just] a pop-up ad?*

Bigman is concerned about the impact this trend may have on journalism and the media. If advertisers essentially figure out how journalism works; that is, how to write articles viewers will read and no longer need the involvement of media companies and professional journalists to attract eyeballs, he fears that such a turn of events will create problems, not only for the media as a business, but for democracy itself, if the result is no independent press. Therefore, he says, "We have to find ways to fund independent, free journalism that doesn't involve advertising."

NATIVE ADERTISING SHOULD
BRING DELIGHT

When it comes to overtly branded content, Bigman's view is that it just annoys everybody reading the publication. "The platforms have evolved, so the advertising needs to evolve as well, so it's not horrible and annoying, [but, instead is] involving and interesting."

To illustrate his point, Bigman compared two ads—the first, an Old Gold cigarette ad from the 1950s that featured a member of the cast of a sponsored variety or game show introducing a pair of dancing Old Gold cigarette packages, sometimes accompanied by a package of matches. In Bigman's view, these ads were not very compelling. Eventually, he says, advertisers got much better at telling a brand's story and conveying its message. They began to understand how television worked and what it was good at, what it was bad at, and the result was ads that nobody minded viewing. Bigman points to the Coca-Cola ad—"I'd like to teach the world to sing"—that appeared at the end of the last episode of *Mad Men* as a great example of that sort of ad. "My daughter's five, and [the other day] she was humming that song [which was launched in 1972] for no apparent reason. . . . It's a happy little ditty, nobody minds [it] and [it became part of] our culture, because it [added value]; and it was beautiful; it was interesting. It wasn't an [in-your-face] X10 ad."

Native advertising is doing the same thing that TV advertisers did. It is their attempt to evolve advertising to meet the demands of the Internet. Bigman acknowledged, "There are going to be some bumps," but, he said, "hopefully there are going to be some beautiful things that come out of it too."

Hearst's Todd Haskell amplifies Bigman's view when he emphasized the importance of creating content that "drives reader delight," which of course is different for every brand. "With a brand like *Harper's Bazaar*, [which is] very visual, it's all about beautiful imagery [so the content of an ad in *Harper's* must comport with that]. With a brand like *Esquire*, [an ad should have] a very different tonality." As Haskell sees it, the best practice is to understand what it is that that reader really responds to and to take that insight and apply it to a branded content program.

CREATE VALUABLE CONTENT

Forbes's Lewis DVorkin has a take on native advertising much like Bigman's and offered some advice to marketers, "We're in the early stages of it. Some of the content [is] good, some of it's not very good, and some of it needs to be improved. Marketers have to learn [not to] try to sell [the viewer] anything. . . . If you're beating someone over the head to sell them something, it's never going to work. [Instead, they should provide] information, [that offers a] perspective that [makes viewers] go, 'Huh, that's pretty interesting,' [not] 'Oh, they're . . . trying to sell me something.' Sell me something won't work. The interesting part will work, and the BrandVoice partners who come to grips with that do very well, and the ones who don't, find that life is difficult."

Some of those who advertise with Forbes do a great job, DVorkin says; among them SAP and NetApp. In his opinion, some at Oracle are doing a good job, "but [others] are still treating it like a public relations marketing thing vs. an information [that offers a unique] perspective. The PR thing is not going to work. The marketing thing is not going to work. The information thing is going to work."

As DVorkin views it, journalists have been doing this kind of writing for 100 years; marketers haven't, they were doing something different. Since native advertising online is so new, relatively speaking, he believes that there are various conflicting or competing influences telling them, "Here's the way you do it," that are affecting how branded content should be handled. Right now, he explains, "They're learning that it's hard to create valuable content in a credible news environment. It's not an easy thing to do. . . . It takes a while. SAP is doing it, but it's been five years now; NetApp, three or four years."

Like Bigman, DVorkin points to the fact that many of the good companies are building their own newsrooms—hiring journalists and other experts. "Here's the reality: I've been in many corporate newsrooms. I've seen newsrooms at ad agencies, and I've seen newsrooms at PR companies. That's the way it's going, their versions of newsrooms creating content on a digital platform." They are doing it because digital publishing meant "everybody could create any content, whatever they wanted to create, at any time they wanted to [create] it. They didn't have to get the newspaper, the magazine, or the TV [station] to allow them to do it [by giving them] space. They could just go do it on the web, and that's what changed everything."

CLEARLY MARK AND VALIDATE CONTENT

Of course, there are still (and always will be) consumers who are very cynical, who will want every article they read online to cite the source of the information it's imparting, so that they can validate it (or ignore it, if it can't be validated). With the blurring of editorial content and advertising, that issue will become even more prevalent. Bigman thinks that's absolutely appropriate; as he put it, "You should always trust but verify, right? I would never advocate people just accept everything they read blindly; there's a reason why the *New York Times* is the *New York Times*, and some other [publications] are less well respected. . . . The people who work on staff [at those well-respected publications] work really, really hard to get it right, and that's why those are credible [publications.]"

He went on to say, "I think some brands [also] work really, really hard, [maybe not to report information per se], but to entertain you or to interest you or give you a new way of looking at the world." In terms of the content itself, Bigman thinks, "As long as it's clearly marked, if it's good, it's good; if it's not good, it's not good."

IDENTIFY BRANDED
CONTENT AT THE TOP

The history of best practices in terms of disclosing what is advertising is interesting. For example, back in the 1960s and 1970s (and possibly even later than that), there were some cases regarding problems identifying ads in print publications. As a result, the FTC mandated that a newspaper ad should always feature the word "advertisement" at the top of the ad. This could appear in very small letters—for example, 8- or 9-point type, which looks like this:

This is 8-point type in this typeface

This is 9-point type in this typeface

While the size of the type was a factor, it was not the critical factor. Instead, what *was* critical was that the word "advertisement" had to appear at the top of any ad, in order not to run afoul of the regulators.

Dan Bigman agrees that the same principle should apply to native advertising. "I think if a brand's affiliated, it should [state] at the top that this was done for or by this brand," but he's concerned about how it is done. "It needs to be done in a way that's respectful to the intelligence of the user or the viewer. People are smarter than we think, and if the government [is mandating disclosure requirements], through the FTC, I think there are more elegant ways of getting across the fact that something is sponsored than [what the FTC is recommending]." If the disclosure is too blatant, Bigman believes that the ads are going to annoy people just as early television ads did. "Wouldn't you rather have [ads] that work and are entertaining [that] potentially [will endure] . . . 30 years from now?" he asks.

Brandtale's Ben Darr sees things a little differently. "As a consumer we've been watching this stuff for a while. It's encouraging to see how the industry has evolved in the last 18 months. Eighteen months ago . . . we didn't see disclosure on a lot of content, and we didn't know [if something was] branded content or not. Did the advertiser pay to have this created or not? And if we are the experts and we, as consumers, couldn't tell, that was really bad. But over the last 18 months, most publishers have gotten their act together and are making it super clear at the top of the article."

BE AWARE OF FTC GUIDELINES

Bill Densmore, now a journalism consultant, who co-owned (with his wife) several weekly newspapers in western Massachusetts that served an area that included southern Vermont, says that they adopted the type of disclosure the FTC promulgated for newspapers:

> We followed that practice when we owned weeklies, and, as suggested by journalism practice and by the FTC, tried to differentiate the typeface and look of an ad so that it didn't look like our editorial content. I thought that was a fair bargain with our readers. The message was, *This is not news; it's somebody else's story, and they're paying us to put it in front of you.*

The FTC didn't *require* publications to mark all their ads with the headline "advertisement"—that is, it wasn't a law—but it was *guidance* from the FTC. In other words, publications and advertisers include it because they don't want to risk having an enforcement action brought against them. Still, sometimes these disclosures blend in so well with the rest of the content in a given publication that it's difficult—really difficult—to tell what is and is not editorial content written by the journalists at the publication and sponsored content provided by some third-party source who is seeking to advertise some product or service. For example, Densmore described this:

> The *New York Times* publishes an advertorial from the government of Russia . . . . about once a month, and it's beautifully

done. . . . Honestly, I forget now how they identify it as advertising. They obviously must somehow, because it's the *New York Times*. You have to have your antennae up when that section comes out to not see it as real content.

And this is the interesting thing, from whose point of view is it not editorial content? I think the government of Russia feels it's totally legitimate editorial content, and their commercial interest is only in promoting the public policy points of view of the Russian state, which is what America does too.

This is a very, very tricky area, but it's an area that journalism has to enter into and consider and offer ethical and business guidance on, and it's particularly made trickier by technology that's available now.

The *Times* current guidelines state (among other guidelines) that the following must appear on all supplements:

- "Slug ADVERTISEMENT must appear horizontally in 8-point Helvetica capitals type or equivalent sans serif, at the upper right and left corners of each page.
- "The following disclaimer must appear on the first page of the advertorial: 'This advertising supplement is produced by [name of sponsor] and did not involve the reporting or editorial staff of the *New York Times*.'"[1]

Where does Densmore believe the FTC will or should go from here? As he perceives them, the FTC information and enforcement policy guidelines are "really comprehensive." As a result, he doesn't think there's much more they can add in terms of recommendations for how businesses should handle native advertising, although as he said above, he does think disclosure is something publications and journalists will have to contend with. In addition, he doesn't think FTC involvement has permanently ended; rather, he concludes, "The FTC's argument is that it's just trying to extend into cyberspace what it has been doing with relatively good acceptance for 30 or 40 years in print and broadcast. I think the challenge is going to be when something is done that doesn't have an obvious parallel [with] what was done in print or broadcast in the past—then what will the FTC do?"

BEST PRACTICES IN PRESENTING NATIVE CONTENT

So what are, and what should be, the best practices media and advertisers should strive for in presenting native content?

Ed McLoughlin at Hewlett-Packard summed it up concisely: "transparency and making sure that it's contextually relevant to the environment it's in; that it's not disrupting their experience. So it feels like it could be part of the content, but [at the same time] people know [that it's not]." He emphasized the need to remain true to the environment the ad is running in when he said, "Just to insert the native content on the page or the mobile platform [won't be enough], it needs to fit with the environment."

"I definitely think," says Heather Dumford of ConAgra, "that a best practice that we've learned through trial and error is [to] create content that stands alone, and that is meant to be experienced as content, [which means] not just . . . throwing an ad into a native unit." She strongly recommends that other advertisers do the same.

While they may not always succeed in living up to that advice, Dumford says, "We definitely strive for it. We never just take our ads off of television and run them as content . . . unless that ad is more [of] what I call Super Bowl–worthy. . . . We put our [TV] content under very tight guidelines and measurements . . . to see if consumers think it's entertaining enough. Then maybe we will [run it in a native ad], but it rarely happens."

Although some native distribution companies she works with have tried to convince her to put ads into native units, she doesn't do it because she believes that if consumers scrolling through a news site or a celebrity gossip site click on a video that has populated the site and finds it is just an ad, they will most likely feel fooled into watching something that they probably wouldn't have. Of course, there is that one exception for "an ad that is truly entertaining, [a] Super Bowl–type ad," but then she adds, "there's not a lot of those out there."

CREATE CONTENT THAT
MATTERS TO CUSTOMERS

With respect to lifestyle publications and news publications, Troy Young at Hearst believes in "disclosing the association in ways that feel right to the environment, . . . so our lockup of created by our brand for another commercial brand makes a lot of sense to me. But . . . the guiding light . . . is finding ways to make the publishing and editorial sides of the house work together so that we can keep creating content that matters to consumers. That's what I really care about. . . . I don't want to undermine our editorial franchises. What I want to do is find new ways to make advertising work so that we can keep making great content."

Young believes it's harder and harder to be an advertiser, because "it's so easy [for viewers] to tune out ads in an on-demand world, and so I think that what's . . . really hard is [finding ways for] advertisers [to] stay relevant. [As I see it, the publisher's] role is to help them make content that consumers care about, and that [getting to] the intersection [where] a commercial message and a piece of marketable editorial [meet] is "really, really hard to do . . . really well."

To him, best practice is when publishers create sponsored or branded or partnered content that performs just as well as pure editorial because that means publishers are serving the consumer and building their businesses. In other words, he explains, "everybody wins. . . . [publishers] earn their audiences every day. When the branded content teams make content that people like, when it's consumed, that's what matters to me."

BE READY FOR NEW DEVELOPMENTS IN MOBILE AND SOCIAL MEDIA

And what does the future hold for native advertising?

"I think that the world of content marketing, native advertising [will] continue to explode on the mobile phone," says Lewis DVorkin. In his view, people want great headlines and great information, and the mobile phone gives them just that. In addition, he points out, it "continues to democratize everything, because [everything is] on the same little screen." He also thinks that . . . journalistic content and native ad content will also have to change to accommodate the size of the real estate. Using BrandVoice as an example, he says you've got native advertising "*here* on a page, and you've got staffer content *here* on a page, and the pages look the same, but [on mobile phones they'll be on] one page; everybody [will be] writing about the same topic on the same page. It's all going to merge."

Although we probably have not yet seen everything there is to see when it comes to native advertising and mobile technology, Liya Sharif of Qualcomm may be envisioning an even more distant future when she said, "I think [native advertising] is going to become more prominent, more pronounced, [and] that native advertising will evolve and expand into a multitude of forms, including social media. . . . Facebook right now [is] publishing . . . instant articles for brands. . . . All the platforms must include some form of native advertising. Snapchat is doing it today, so it's becoming a de facto in the industry, one of the tactics for brands to position themselves deeper." Sharif sees it as a "classic expansion" of native advertising from one platform to another.

Thinking along similar lines, Steve Piluso also cited social media, especially Instagram, which includes "stuff that isn't overtly called out as native advertising" but is nevertheless interesting, especially to advertising and marketing professionals. He pointed to one example:

> I've started following Kylie Jenner on Instagram, because she incorporates her own brand a lot in a very natural way. I've noticed she's always wearing Puma shoes and Puma athletic gear. So she's obviously being paid by Puma to do that, but

it doesn't seem unnatural. It's a brand that really fits with her and her lifestyle. . . .

I'm seeing more and more of that. I'm seeing brands use Instagram really well that way, [although] I don't know if that's "native advertising" or a celebrity endorsement, but it certainly is weaving a brand into the fabric of [the] narrative behind every photo. Every picture tells a story. The fact that brands are being woven into that narrative in a way that seems really natural and smart I think is great.

While Piluso thinks Jenner's association with Puma products seems entirely natural, he also pointed out that if she were seen on Instagram using a product like PAM® cooking spray (his example), he's confident that consumers would recognize that this was contrived (he used more colorful language to describe it). The bottom line is that the product association needs to be "the right match."

Piluso is fascinated by how brands are utilizing the advertising opportunities on Instagram. "If I were an 18- to 24-year-old girl and I thought Kylie Jenner was fantastic, I can certainly see how I'd be considering Puma a lot more than, say, Skechers or some other brand that's a little more prominent and advertising forward. So I like that stuff. I think it's interesting."

GROW INTO NEW
BRANDED EXPERIENCES

From an industry perspective, Ben Darr of Brandtale finds it really interesting to see how much branded content is being created and how it's grown over the last 18 months. He thinks brands are starting to get a little smarter now about how they spend their money. "Instead of working with 20 or 30 or 40 different publishing partners every year," he explains, "they're starting to learn who they can work with best, where they should be devoting their time and effort, and they're starting to pick the four or five publishing partners that they want to go all in with and spend most of their money with." He believes that's a product of how difficult it is to actually produce good branded content and how much easier it is to do if you work with a small subset of people.

Another thing to take note of in this whole shift to branded content, Darr says, is that we're starting to see publishers create experiences and investigative reports that they never would have created before, because brands are giving them the budget to go and do it.

"Branded content is [giving] consumers editorial experiences that they never would have gotten without [it], because publishers, a lot of the time, don't have the budget to do the awesome and crazy reports and experiences that they [might] want to do. . . . So brands are actually fueling a lot of the investigative reports and awesome experiences [we see on television]." Darr recognizes that brand sponsorship can also be dangerous, because the brand might have an ulterior motive in sponsoring some of these investigative reports, but, he says, when it doesn't or when brands underwrite less serious content and more pure entertainment, "there's huge value-added for the consumer." He points to a serious collaboration between Netflix and the *Wall Street Journal* on a show called *Coconomics*, about the economics behind the cocaine trade and Pablo Escobar, which he thinks made a lot of sense.

Even when you compare a lot of the branded content to normal articles, he adds, "You'll see the branded content has a lot more special design, greater technological sophistication, and product treatment than normal content, because brands want to put money into the experience."

INVEST WITH PARTNERS IN AN OVERALL GREAT EXPERIENCE FOR THE CONSUMER

Jason Loehr at Brown-Forman may unwittingly have summed up the current and future state of successful native advertising—regardless of medium or format—for publishers and advertisers alike, when he said:

> I think it's about investing the time in [your] partner to make sure that [together you create] an overall great experience for the consumer. The other piece of that is [the requirement to] recognize the context and transparency that's needed. People sometimes aren't given enough credit to recognize [branded content when they see it]—*of course I know this is a paid sponsorship.* . . . At the end of the day, it's making sure that the content itself really stands on its own. . . . That's [such an] important thing, because if the content is great, great stories will always win.

ACKNOWLEDGMENTS

I want to acknowledge and express my appreciation for the many people who helped to make this book possible.

To my partner on this book, Ruth Mills. I value my collaboration with Ruth very much and I am grateful to Ruth for her contributions, her good nature, and her professionalism.

To Lori Ames, for her guidance throughout this project and for helping me with publicity, marketing, and public relations.

I am grateful to Dana Newman, my literary agent, for her expert guidance.

I am also grateful to the wonderful team at my publisher, McGraw-Hill Education: Donya Dickerson, Pattie Amoroso, Peter McCurdy, Maureen Harper, and Steve Straus.

I am grateful to the people who agreed to be interviewed for *The Native Advertising Advantage*: Troy Young, Kate Lewis, Todd Haskell, Meredith Levien, Lewis DVorkin, Rebecca Babcock, Hilary Batsel, Dan Bigman, Michael Brenner, Alexa Christon, Julia Claflin, Francesca Conlin, Ben Darr, Bill Densmore, Felix DiFilippo, Charles Dubow, Heather Dumford, John Ferber, Dan Greenberg, Keith Griffith, Elizabeth Hansen, Eric Jillard, Adam Kasper, Jason Kint, Luke Kintigh, Jason Loehr, Ed McLoughlin, Dhawal Mujumdar, Steve Piluso, Satish Polisetti, Jeff Ratner,

Avinoam Rubinstain, Liya Sharif, Adam Shlachter, Jeff Sternstein, Derek Topel, Adam Singolda, and Jay Widlitz.

To my supportive family: my wife, Denise, and our children, Jessica and Michael; my late parents Edward and Patricia Smith; my brother Dave and his family (Vicky, Harry, Eddie, and Devon); my brother Joe and his family (Melanie, Chris, Alex, and Maddy); my mother-in-law, Darlene Manfra; my father-in-law and his wife, Ray and Barbara Manfra; and my brother-in-law, Ray Manfra, and his family (Jennifer and Amanda).

I have the good fortune of working at Hearst and would like to thank my colleagues for their support on this project: Troy Young, Phil Wiser, David Carey, Debi Chirichella, Lincoln Millstein, Michael Clinton, Steven R. Swartz, Will Hearst, Mitch Scherzer, Eve Burton, Jeff Hamill, Jordan Wertlieb, Mark Aldam, Neeraj Khemlani, Nick Brien, Mike Racic, Simon Horne, Giacomo Moletto, Robert Schoenmaker, Luc Van Os, Todd Haskell, Kate Lewis, Jack Rohan, Kenan Packman, Gabby Munoz, Michael Benham, Roger Keating, Jon Sumber, Rob Barrett, Karen Brophy and Debra Robinson.

To my assistants who supported me during this book project: Porsche Bradberry and Savannah Shipman.

To Hearst's communications team: Debra Shriver, Paul Luthringer, Alex Carlin, Grace Stearns and Sheila O'Shea.

To Ravi Sitwala in Hearst Legal for his expert guidance.

To DKC's Jeffrey Klein, Nazli Ekim, Marni Raitt, Maayan Weiss, and Meredith Obendorfer.

To the late Joyce Newman.

To my colleagues at Hearst U.K. who taught me a great deal about content marketing and branded content: James Wildman,

Anna Jones, Claire Blunt, Michael Rowley, Surinder Simmons, Clare Gorman, Guljeet Samra, Duncan Chater, Paul Cassar, Vic White, Ali Gray, Aimee Nisbet, Lisa Quinn, Hayley Cochrane, Ben Giles, Dan Levitt, Tracy Yaverbaun, Dani Klein, Simon Reed, Jane Wolfson, Judith Secombe, Di Thorpe, Victoria Archbold, Reid Holland, Tanya Stewart, Rikki Embley, Natasha Mann, Elly Bobard, Roisin Edwards, Jai Grant-Samuels, Julien Litzelmann and Darren Goldsby.

To Victor Shkulev of Hearst Shkulev Media.

To friends Jim Spanfeller, John Taysom, Roger McNamee, Dave Moore, Jim Flock, Albie Collins, and Kevin English.

The Forbes family has been very kind to me. I would like to express my gratitude to Moira Forbes, Steve Forbes, Tim Forbes, Bob Forbes, Kip Forbes, Wally Forbes, and Miguel Forbes.

To Forbes colleagues Mike Perlis, Mike Federle, Achir Kalra, Mark Howard, Tom Davis, Bruce Rogers, Michael Dugan, and Christina Vega.

To friends and colleagues Hayley Romer, Beth Buehler, John French, Sharon Gitelle-French, and Jonah Goodhart.

I learned a great deal about content marketing by listening to PnR's "This Old Marketing" podcast every Monday. Joe Pulizzi and Robert Rose are content marketing experts, and I would like to acknowledge their positive influence on my work.

To my colleagues at Hearst: Julie Clark, Ali Abelson, Scott Both, Heather Keltz, Weyland Jung, Dave Strauss, Charles Wolrich, and Greta Lawn. Brooke Edwards, Jessica Mason, Kelsey Woo, Jason Tsang, Amy Weinstein, Andrew Grant, and Tony Park. Scherri Roberts, Joe Farrell, and Ali Fink. Jenny Erasmus, Jessica Seibert, Anne Stolzer, Kristin Zinkler, Lauren Pfeiffer, Lisa

Hermes, Nicole Guba, Reggie Louis-Jacques, Stephanie Capone, Michelle Clemente, Juliana Lustig, Stephanie Oliveri, Kristi Zhang, Gina Nchekwube, Jessica Peterson, Nzingha Ford, Sam Meiczkowsa, Justin Love, Arani Sen, Joanne Jantzen, Kristin Denison, Michelle Landi, Jamie Luther, Jordan Randazzo, Kelly Carpenter, Annabelle Gould, Christina Buttafuoco, Gavin Davids, Bethany Devendorf, Rachel Franchella, Annabelle Gould, Michael Hall, Joanne Jantzen, Sionna Kelly, Juliana Lustig, Meagan Maginot, Christina Manzi, Matt Milligan, Tom Mokrzecki, Arianna Nacci, Antoniette Pemberton, Jessica Peterson, Emily Tan, Meagan Greene, Jeff Early, Kim Betrus, Laurel Coimer, Sarah Kahn, Janet Yungwirth, Tonie Pemberton, Joelle Krakower, Amanda Wood, Gab Vaccaro, Kristin Zinkler. Elizabeth Baisley, Kevin Bowen, Daniel Brathwaite, Suzi Brown, Angel Burney, Melissa Campedelli, Roy Cerrillo, Lauren Cordes, Taylor Couchois, Annikah Ewen, Robert Flowers, Rachel Friedman, Brendan Garrone, Carly Goodwin, Bobby Hayes, Adam Javorsky, Amy Jiang, Alison Johnston, Catherine Kennedy, Ronny Lai, Jack Lin, Richard Marr, Jennifer McAuliffe, Elizabeth McLarty, Charles Mitchell, Dave Morin, Elizabeth Meyers, Anthony Polcino, Derek Roberts, Martina Rogers, Kate Sloan, Nick Van Winkle, Angelo Vrachnas, Pete Vredenburgh, Monica Stinson, John Branco, and Gareth Yiu. Heather Arouh, Laura Kalehoff, Lee Sosin, Jason Kleinman, Brian Madden, Michael Mraz, Kayvan Salmanpour, Theresa Mershon, Amy Laine, Allison Keane, Steve McNally, Sheel Shah, Jim Mortko, Ed Urgola, Brooke Siegel, and Sam Mansour. Brittany Cherichella, Debra Phillip, Michael Mangano, and Brian Murray.

Rich Antoniello, Jennifer Yousem, Scott Cherkin, Moksha Fitzgibbons, and Jeetu Chawla at Complex Media.

NOTES

FOREWORD

1. http://www.pewglobal.org/2016/02/22/smartphone-ownership
-rates-skyrocket-in-many-emerging-economies-but-digital-divide
-remains/

INTRODUCTION

1. Kelsey Libert, "Comparing the ROI of Content Marketing and NA" *Harvard Business Review*, July 6, 2015.
2. Jack Neff, "Is It Content or Is It Advertising?" *AdvertisingAge*, October 12, 2015.
3. Ibid.
4. The terms *branded content* and *sponsored content* are often used interchangeably.
5. *The 2014 Native Advertising Roundup*, as cited in "Everything You Need to Know About Sponsored Content, " Chad Pollitt, https://moz.com/blog/everything-you-need-to-know-about-sponsored
-content, January 20, 2015.
6. Margaret Boland, "Native Ads Will Drive 74% of All Ad Revenue by 2021," Business Insider/*BIIntelligence*, June 14, 2016.
7. *The 2014 Native Advertising Roundup*, as cited in "Everything You Need to Know About Sponsored Content."
8. Ibid.
9. Copyblogger.com, "2014 State of Native Advertising Report," as cited in "Everything You Need to Know About Sponsored Content."

CHAPTER 1

1. from an interview with Charles Dubow
2. from an interview with Dhawal Mujumdar
3. from an interview with Satish Polisetti
4. from an interview with Jeff Sternstein
5. from an interview with Heather Dumford
6. Todd Wasserman, "What Is 'Native Advertising'? Depends Who You Ask," mashable.com, September 25, 2012.
7. Dilip Mutum and QingWang, "Consumer Generated Advertising in Blogs," in Neal M. Burns, Terry Daugherty, and Matthew S. Eastin, *Handbook of Research on Digital Media and Advertising: User Generated Content Consumption* (IGI Global, 2010), 248–261, as quoted on Wikipedia.
8. Anders Vinderslev, "The Top 10 Examples of BuzzFeed Doing Native Advertising," Native Advertising Institute, September 30, 2015, http://nativeadvertisinginstitute.com/blog/the-top-10 -examples-of-buzzfeed-doing-native-advertising/.
9. StackAdapt, "IAB Native Advertising Playbook," March 16, 2015, http://blog.stackadapt.com/iab-native-advertising-playbook.
10. "The Six Core Types of Native Ads," http://flite.com/blog-post/ home/2014/3/25/the-six-core-types-of-native-ads.
11. "The IAB Native Advertising Playbook," December 4, 2013, 2 (emphasis mine).
12. Ibid., 3 (emphasis in the original).
13. "Native advertising," Wikipedia, https://en.m.wikipedia.org/wiki/ Native_advertising.
14. Wikipedia.
15. Felix Salmon, quoted in Tony Hallett, "What Is Native Advertising Anyway?" TheGuardian.com.
16. from an interview with Satish Polisetti
17. from an interview with Satish Polisetti
18. from an interview with Charles Dubow
19. from an interview with Dan Bigman
20. Oracle BrandVoice article, no longer available online.
21. from an interview with Dan Bigman
22. "Forbes Achieves New Milestone—100 BrandVoice Partners," Forbes Corporate Communications, September 8, 2015, http:// www.forbes.com/sites/forbespr/2015/09/08/forbes-achieves-new -milestone-over-100-brandvoice-partners/#5d123a68465b.

23. http://www.politico.com/about/press/facts.
24. http://www.politico.com/magazine/sponsor-generated-content.
25. from an interview with Dan Bigman
26. "The IAB Native Advertising Playbook," December 4, 2013, "The NA Playbook" (white paper).
27. Sharethrough, "Native Advertising Insights: Research, Infographics and Resources," http://www.sharethrough.com/nativeadvertising/, accessed August 13, 2016.

CHAPTER 2

1. Martin Bryant, "20 Years Ago Today, the World Wide Web Opened to the Public," TNW, August 6, 2011, http://thenextweb .com/insider/2011/08/06/20-years-ago-today-the-world-wide-web -opened-to-the-public/.
2. Cameron Chapman, "The History of the Internet in a Nutshell," Six Revisions, n.d., http://sixrevisions.com/resources/the-history-of -the-internet-in-a-nutshell/.
3. Robert W. McChesney, *Digital Disconnect: How Capitalism Is Turning the Internet Against Democracy* (New York: The New Press, 2013).
4. from an interview with Dan Bigman
5. from an interview with Dan Bigman
6. from an interview with Charles Dubow
7. Young
8. John McDuling, "BuzzFeed Is Killing It, and Its Older Rivals Are Rattled," Quartz, December 14, 2014.
9. "Why Are Journalists Hostile to Forbes' Lewis DVorkin? He Wants Them to Get Real," Pando, April 18, 2013, https://pando .com/2013/04/18/why-are-journalists-hostile-to-forbes-lewis -dvorkin-he-wants-them-to-get-real/.
10. Aaron Smith, "U.S. Smartphone Use in 2015," Pew Research Center, April 1, 2015, http://www.pewinternet.org/2015/04/01/us -smartphone-use-in-2015/.

CHAPTER 3

1. Michael Wolff, "Even the *New York Times* Can't Resist Going Low-brow with Native Advertising," theguardian.com, December 23, 2013.
2. Brian Braiker, "Andrew Sullivan on Native Ads: Journalism Has Surrendered," digiday.com, May 7, 2014.
3. Remarks of Linda Fantin Miller, director of the Public Insight Network at American Public Media, as transcribed by Bill Densmore, moderator of the event "RJI Five Past/Five Forward," September 10, 2013, at the Donald W. Reynolds Journalism Institute, Missouri School of Journalism, Columbia, Missouri. Found at http://www.youtube.com/watch?v=vYDmEc5F-6c (starts at 20:25).
4. "The *Atlantic* Advertising Guidelines," http://cdn.theatlantic.com/static/front/docs/ads/TheAtlanticAdvertisingGuidelines.pdf.
5. Taylor Berman, "The *Atlantic* Is Now Publishing Bizarre, Blatant Scientology Propaganda as 'Sponsored Content,'" Gawker.com, January 14, 2013.
6. Erik Wemple, "The *Atlantic*'s Scientology Problem, Start to Finish," *Washington Post*, January 15, 2013.
7. Ibid.
8. James Fallows, "The *Atlantic*: The Scientology Ad," theatlantic.com, January 15, 2013.
9. Amanda Walgrove, "The NYT Just Created an Incredible 'Snow Fall' for 'Orange Is the New Black,'" contently.com, June 13, 2014.
10. Kissmetrics, "How to Evaluate the ROI of Branded Content."

CHAPTER 4

1. see http://www.spj.org/ethicscode.asp.
2. "The IAB Native Advertising Playbook," December 4, 2013.
3. Ibid.
4. Ibid., 15.
5. Sarah Sluis, "FTC: Publishers Will Be Held Responsible for Misleading Native Ads," June 3, 2015, http://adexchanger.com.
6. Ibid.
7. U.S. Federal Trade Commission, "Enforcement Policy Statement on Deceptively Formatted Advertisements," December 22, 2015.
8. Ibid., 2–3.
9. Ibid., 8.

10. "IAB Concerned about FTC Guidance on Native Advertising," www.iab.com, December 24, 2015.

CHAPTER 5

1. Believe it or not, that's true. The first personal computers arrived on office desks in the mid-1980s, so most writers more than 50 years old were still typing on electric typewriters in the early years of their careers.

CHAPTER 6

1. Michael Sebastian, "Nearly Two-Thirds of Marketers Plan to Increase Native-Ad Spending in 2015, But Native Remains a Small Fraction of Budgets," *Advertising Age*, January 29, 2015.
2. Michelle Castillo, "How HP Turned 6-Second Vines into a 30-Second TV Ad: Brands Are Repurposing Social Media, Memes into Multi-platform Campaigns," *Adweek*, October 27, 2014.
3. Michael del Castillo, "GE to Ride Google Cardboard into a New Era of Virtual Reality Advertising," *New York Business Journal*, November 4, 2015.
4. Anders Vinderslev, "Marriott Hotels Wins Native Advertising Award with Innovative Reddit Campaign," Native Advertising Institute, May 5, 2015.
5. Humira TV Spot, "Body of Proof," https://www.ispot.tv/ad/ADg0/humira-body-of-proof.
6. Chris Sutcliffe, "Transparency and Quality: Approaches to Native Ads from Quartz and GE," October 1, 2014, www.themediabriefing.com.
7. Sydney Ember, "General Electric Planning Television Series Covering Science and Tech," *New York Times*, April 13, 2015.
8. Ibid.
9. Ibid.
10. Saya Weissman, "GE Takes a Deep Dive into Native Advertising," digiday.com, March 31, 2014.
11. Jack Hershman, "Pepsi CMO: Why Advertising Should Be More Like the *Empire* Campaign," www.hottopics.ht/stories/advertising/inside-pepsi-native-advertising-strategy/.

12. "Intel and Lady Gaga Come Together for an Amazing Music Experience at the 58th Annual Grammy® Awards," February 15, 2016, https://newsroom.intel.com/news-releases/.
13. Full disclosure: *Esquire* is a Hearst magazine.
14. Tim Calkins, "Cadillac's Curious Start," Kellogg School of Management, March 5, 2015, www.timcalkins.com.
15. Jonny Lieberman, "Four-Door Miracles: The State of the Art Is on Fire," *Motor Trend*, August 1, 2015.
16. Cadillac, "Invisible Innovations Are Transforming the Way We Live, Work, and Engage with One Another" (Cadillac sponsor content), Quartz, http://qz.com/701869/interactive-the-ideas-shaping-everything-from-your-kitchen-to-your-city/.

CHAPTER 7

1. *The 2014 Native Advertising Roundup*, as cited in "Everything You Need to Know About Sponsored Content." January 20, 2015, https://moz.com/blog/everything-you-need-to-know-about-sponsored-content.
2. "Branded-Content Sites Deliver Better Ad Results," Watershield Publishing, as cited in Wikipedia definition of "Branded Content."
3. Mike Shields, "Native Advertising Tech Firm Nativo Raises $20 Million in New Funding," WSJ.com, June 30, 2015.
4. Emphasis is mine.

CHAPTER 8

1. *The New York Times* Advertising Acceptability Manual, revised January 2015, http://nytmediakit.com/uploads/specs/NYT_Digital_Ad_Acceptability_Guidelines.pdf.

INDEX

on authenticity, 41
on branded content and native
  advertising, 12
on brand permission, 64–65
on future developments, 180
on native advertising, 26, 66
on women inmates article, 59–61
Pinterest, 124–125
Placement, 11, 64–66
Policy-focused brands, 114
Polisetti, Satish, 65–66, 80–81
Politico, 18–20
Pop-up ads, 30
Post-it products, 99–100, 166
Prescribing information, 83, 84
Presenting native content, 177–178
Print publications:
  added value of advertising in,
    153–154
  advertorials in, 27–29
  brands' native advertising in,
    144–149
  divide between editorial and
    advertising in, 2
  FTC guidelines for, 173–175
Product placement, 27
Promoted listings, 7, 75–76
Promoted tweets (Twitter), 9, 86
Promoted videos, 9
Publishers:
  disclosure guidelines for, 74–82
  distinguishing editorial vs.
    advertising content, 68–69
  distinguishing sponsored from
    journalistic content, 69–74
  financial necessities for, 95
  implementation of native
    advertising by, 14–22
  transparency by, 68–74
Puma, 180–181
PureWow, 138

Qualcomm, 42–44, 130–131
Quartz, 126, 130–131, 148

Radio advertising, 26
Ratner, Jeff, 34–35, 38–39, 81–82,
  132
Recommendation widgets, 6–7, 75
Red Bull, 22–23
Reddit, 120

Refinery29, 142
Regulated industries, challenges for,
  83–88
Retail industry, 114, 115
Revenue from native advertising, xiv
Road & Track, 52
Russian government advertorials,
  175–176

Sales pitches, 77
Salmon, Felix, 12
SAP, 17, 171, 172
Scientology article, 56–58
Scrubbing bubbles, 107
Search ads, 6, 75, 158, 168
Sharethrough, 4, 9
Sharif, Liya, 20, 42–44, 131, 180
Shlachter, Adam:
  on branded content and native
    advertising, 12
  on brands' native advertising, 133,
    134, 136–137
  concerns/complaints about native
    advertising, 165
TheSkimm.com, 159–160
Slim Jim, 122–123, 125, 126
Smartphones, 48–50
Snapchat, 50, 180
Social influencers, 116–118
Social media:
  advertising on, 132
  consumer profiles on, 86–87
  readiness for new developments in,
    179–181
Software developers, 13
Southern Comfort, 87, 109–111
Spark, 43
Spending on native advertising, xiv,
  108–109 (*See also* Budgets for
  native advertising)
Spiriva, 121, 122
Sponsored content, 11
  distinguishing journalistic content
    from, 69–74
  in early years, 31
  impact of, 152
  native advertising vs., 3
  (See also Branded content)
Sponsored posts, 5, 8–10
Sports Illustrated, 58
Spotify, 7, 9

ABOUT THE AUTHOR

Mike Smith is Senior Vice President of Revenue Platforms and Operations, Hearst Magazines Digital Media as well as Senior Vice President Advertising Platforms of Hearst's Core Audience. Smith joined Hearst in July 2013 and is responsible for all digital media revenue platforms, including the company's programmatic sales engineering efforts through the Hearst Audience Exchange as well as advertising operations and digital ad product development.

Prior to Hearst, Smith held a number of positions with Forbes, most recently as the President of Forbes.com and Chief Digital Officer of Forbes Media, where he oversaw the company's technology departments, including IT systems, multi-platform development and digital strategy. He was also responsible for audience sales via auctions including trading desks, advertising operations, data and analytics, and yield management.

Before joining Forbes.com as Chief Technology Officer, Smith was Vice President and Chief Information Officer at TheStreet .com, where he directed technology efforts, including application development, network engineering, website operations, global technology initiatives and business support systems. Prior to that, he was Director of Information Technology at HBO.

Smith holds a network-technology related patent and is the author of the book *TARGETED: How Technology Is Revolutionizing Advertising and the Way Companies Reach Consumers* (AMACOM/2014).

Smith graduated from the New Jersey Institute of Technology with a B.S. in Electrical Engineering and has been a member of the Board of Visitors of NJIT's Albert Dorman Honors College for 14 years, as well as the chairman of the Board of Trustees of the Education Law Center, a member of the School Consultative Board of Union Catholic High School and a member of The Union League Club.

Mike Smith is a lifelong resident of Scotch Plains, New Jersey, where he lives with his wife, Denise, and two children, Jessica and Michael.